This volume investigates the respective theologies of the Letters to the Colossians and the Ephesians, and in so doing provides an accessible introduction to the themes and significance of these New Testament books. A. J. M. Wedderburn examines the background to Colossians, and considers both its readers' situation and that of its author. In this the question of the interpretation of the letter, made more acute by the author's use of traditional material which may have differed in its outlook from his own, and of the theological relevance of the letter, particularly for Christology, are investigated. Andrew T. Lincoln examines in turn the authorship of Ephesians, and tries to explain the letter's strategy of persuasion and the key elements of its teaching about the new identity of the Christian believer. The similarities and differences between the thought of Ephesians and that of Paul are thereby set out clearly. Both sections of the book reflect on the relevance of these letters for today.

# NEW TESTAMENT THEOLOGY

General Editor: James D. G. Dunn,
Lightfoot Professor of Divinity, University of Durham

The theology of the later Pauline letters

This series provides a programmatic survey of the individual writings of the New Testament. It aims to remedy the deficiency of available published material, which has tended to concentrate on historical, textual, grammatical, and literary issues at the expense of the theology, or to lose distinctive emphases of individual writings in systematised studies of 'The Theology of Paul' and the like. New Testament specialists here write at greater length than is usually possible in the introductions to commentaries or as part of other New Testament theologies, and explore the theological themes and issues of their chosen books without being tied to a commentary format, or to a thematic structure drawn from elsewhere. When complete, the series will cover all the New Testament writings, and will thus provide an attractive, and timely, range of texts around which courses can be developed.

# THE THEOLOGY OF THE
# LATER PAULINE LETTERS

## ANDREW T. LINCOLN
*Lecturer in Biblical Studies, University of Sheffield*

## A. J. M. WEDDERBURN
*Lecturer in Theology, University of Durham*

**CAMBRIDGE**
UNIVERSITY PRESS

Published by the Press Syndicate of the University of Cambridge
The Pitt Building, Trumpington Street, Cambridge CB2 1RP
40 West 20th Street, New York, NY 10011–4211, USA
10 Stamford Road, Oakleigh, Victoria, 3166, Australia

First published 1993

Printed in Great Britain at the University Press, Cambridge

*A catalogue record for this book is available from the British Library*

*Library of Congress cataloguing in publication data*

Lincoln, Andrew T.
The theology of the later Pauline letters / Andrew T. Lincoln,
A. J. M. Wedderburn.
p. cm. – (New Testament theology)
Includes bibliographical references.
ISBN 0–521–36460–4 (hardback) – ISBN 0–521–36721–2 (paperback)
1. Bible. N.T. Colossians – Theology. 2. Bible. N.T.
Colossians – Criticism, interpretation, etc. 3. Bible. N.T.
Ephesians – Theology. 4. Bible. N.T. Ephesians – Criticism,
Interpretation, etc. 1. Wedderburn, A. J. M. 11. Title.
111. Series
BS2715.5.L56 1993
227′.506–dc20    92–31674 CIP

ISBN 0 521 36460 4 hardback
ISBN 0 521 36721 2 paperback

# Contents

# Editor's preface

Although the New Testament is usually taught within Departments or Schools or Faculties of Theology/Divinity/Religion, theological study of the individual New Testament writings is often minimal or at best patchy. The reasons for this are not hard to discern.

For one thing, the traditional style of studying a New Testament document is by means of straight exegesis, often verse by verse. Theological concerns jostle with interesting historical, textual, grammatical and literary issues, often at the cost of the theological. Such exegesis is usually very time-consuming, so that only one or two key writings can be treated in any depth within a crowded three-year syllabus.

For another, there is a marked lack of suitable textbooks round which courses could be developed. Commentaries are likely to lose theological comment within a mass of other detail in the same way as exegetical lectures. The section on the theology of a document in the Introduction to a commentary is often very brief and may do little more than pick out elements within the writing under a sequence of headings drawn from systematic theology. Excursuses usually deal with only one or two selected topics. Likewise larger works on New Testament Theology usually treat Paul's letters as a whole and, having devoted the great bulk of their space to Jesus, Paul and John, can spare only a few pages for others.

In consequence, there is little incentive on the part of teacher or student to engage with a particular New Testament document, and students have to be content with a general overview, at best complemented by in-depth study of (parts of) two or three New Testament writings. A serious corollary to this is the degree to which students are thereby incapacitated in the task of integrating their New Testament study with the rest of their Theology or Religion courses, since often they are capable only of drawing on the general overview or on a sequence of particular verses treated atomistically. The growing importance of a literary-critical approach to individual documents simply highlights the present deficiencies even more. Having been given little experience in handling individual New Testament writings as such at a theological level, most students are very ill-prepared to develop a properly integrated literary and theological response to particular texts. Ordinands too need more help than they currently receive from textbooks, so that their preaching from particular passages may be better informed theologically.

There is need therefore for a series to bridge the gap between too brief an introduction and too full a commentary where theological discussion is lost among too many other concerns. It is our aim to provide such a series. That is, a series where New Testament specialists are able to write at a greater length on the theology of individual writings than is usually possible in the introductions to commentaries or as part of New Testament Theologies, and to explore the theological themes and issues of these writings without being tied to a commentary format or to a thematic structure provided from elsewhere. The volumes seek both to describe each document's theology, and to engage theologically with it, noting also its canonical context and any specific influence it may have had on the history of Christian faith and life. They are directed at those who already have one or two years of full-time New Testament and theological study behind them.

James D. G. Dunn
University of Durham

# Note on citations

The conventions of the *Journal of Biblical Literature* 107 (1988) 579–96 are used. Second or subsequent citations of works listed in the guides to further reading are simply cited by an abbreviated title.

# The Theology of Colossians
A. J. M. Wedderburn

# CHAPTER I

# The background of Colossians

Much of the language and many of the ideas of Colossians perhaps strike the twentieth-century reader as puzzling; many of the terms and phrases are obscure, even in the original Greek. If it is in general true of the New Testament letters that the better we understand the situation which led to their being written, the better we understand them, then this is all the more true of Colossians. So we shall need to look with even greater care at what we know of the background to this letter than may be necessary with at least some other New Testament writings, and to consider both its readers' situation and that of the author. And it should not be forgotten that we are often as much influenced by views which we reject as we are by views which we espouse. The author of Colossians is no exception: it is perhaps as important to understand something about those against whom the letter is written, and in response to whom its theology is developed, as it is to know something of the traditions which are endorsed, adopted and adapted by its author.

## THE COLOSSIAN 'HERESY' AND ITS BACKGROUND

For the most part it is assumed that the letter to the Colossians was written to combat some specific set of beliefs and practices that was being propagated in the church in the city of Colossae. That view has been challenged by M. D. Hooker because of the 'calm' with which the writer confronts this threat and the lack of a clear refutation of this false teaching. Is it not more plausible, she asks, that we have here 'a situation in

3

which young Christians are under pressure to conform to the beliefs and practices of their pagan and Jewish neighbours'? This need not be an explicit 'false teaching' current in the Colossian Church, but merely the threat of 'the pressures of the pagan environment' in which they lived, coupled with 'pressure from Jews or Jewish Christians'.[1]

This alternative has not found much favour, and against it is the very specificity of the polemical references in Colossians, at times so specific in fact that we are at a loss to be sure of the exact meaning of phrases like 'taking his stand on visions' (2.18, RSV).[2] If the polemic is not as passionate as Paul's in Galatians or 2 Corinthians, then the explanation may be, not that Colossians is not a polemic against a particular viewpoint, but that the polemic does not come directly from the hand of Paul.[3] It was, anyway, Paul's wont to be less vituperative in admonishing his converts than when criticizing outsiders who were interfering in his churches.

However, one might argue that a specific threat is unlikely because of the sheer variety of the suggestions proposed, which range from Pharisees to Gnostics or adherents of the pagan mystery cults.[4] How are we to choose between these suggestions? (We must recall how important it is for the understanding of this, or any, letter to know as exactly as possible what circumstances occasioned its writing.)

The letter itself gives us a few clues. For a start, the writer of the letter warns its readers against being led astray by 'philosophy' (2.8), and this might be thought to be evidence in

[1] 'Were There False Teachers at Colossae?', in *Christ and Spirit in the New Testament*, ed. B. Lindars and S. S. Smalley, *Festschrift* for C. F. D. Moule (Cambridge University Press, 1973), pp. 313–31, esp. pp. 316, 323, 328.
[2] See n. 25 below.
[3] It will be assumed in this study that Colossians is not written directly by Paul, which is now the general consensus of scholars, at least on the other side of the English Channel, although it may have been written while Paul was still alive (but imprisoned and therefore unable to communicate much with the outside world himself?) and by a close associate of his; cf. A. J. M. Wedderburn, *Baptism and Resurrection: Studies in Pauline Theology against Its Graeco-Roman Background*, WUNT 44 (Tübingen, Mohr, 1987), pp. 70–1 and reff. in n. 10.
[4] See the brief list in M. Kiley, *Colossians as Pseudepigraphy* (Sheffield, JSOT, 1986), pp. 61–2.

support of E. Schweizer's comparison of the Colossian 'heresy' with the account of Pythagorean doctrine given by Alexander Polyhistor (first century BCE) and quoted by Diogenes Laertius (8.24–33).[5] Certainly the contents of this account offer some suggestive parallels or possible parallels with our letter, quite apart from the fact that they are 'philosophy'. From the twin first principles (*archai*; cf. Col. 1.16, 19; 2.10, 15), the monad and the dyad, are ultimately derived the things in this world, formed from four elements (*stoicheia*; cf. Col. 2.8, 20), fire, water, earth and air (§25). The heavenly bodies, sun, moon and stars, are gods (§27). Souls are immortal, and when they leave the body they are stewarded by Hermes, the pure being taken to the heavenly and divine upper region, 'but the impure are not permitted to approach the pure or each other, but are bound by the Furies in bonds unbreakable' (§31). The air is full of souls who are *daimones* and heroes, sending dreams and portents to the people and animals in this world (§32 – these mediating figures or the Furies could very easily be compared with angels by those used to the Judaeo-Christian tradition; cf. Col. 2.18). Purification comes by cleansing, baths and lustrations, by avoiding contact with death and birth and every defilement, and by abstinence from various foodstuffs (meat, eggs, beans, etc.) and 'the other abstinences prescribed by those who perform mystic rites in the temples' (§33).

The abstinence practised by the Pythagoreans invites comparison with various aspects of the position criticized by Colossians, in particular the prohibitions of touching and eating, and the denial of the body's desires mentioned in 2.21–3. It would be tempting, too, to compare the writer's exhortation in 2.16 that the Colossians should not let themselves be judged in respect of food and drink, but that list goes on to mention the observance of festivals, new moons and sabbaths.[6] The last item

---

[5] This is most easily accessible in R. D. Hicks' translation (quoted here) of the *Lives of Eminent Philosophers*, LCL (London, Heinemann, 1925), vol. 2, pp. 340–9. Cf. E. Schweizer, *The Letter to the Colossians: a Commentary* (London, SPCK, 1982; ET of EKKNT (Zürich, etc., Benziger/Neukirchen, Neukirchener, 1976)), p. 132.

[6] This triad is found in almost identical terms in the LXX of 1 Chr. 23.31; 2 Chr. 2.3; 31.3; Hos. 2.13 and Ezek. 45.17, where it quite clearly refers to Jewish rites; cf. Isa. 1.13.

in this list is the clearest evidence which we have that there is a Jewish element in the position against which the writer is contending and that it may not just be 'a pagan philosophy with some Jewish influence'.[7] We do well to recall how widespread ascetic practices were amongst various groups of that day, and to reflect, too, how widespread was the claim to be a 'philosophy'; it is, for instance, used by Philo of Alexandria and other Greek-speaking Jews to describe Judaism.[8]

Thus it is also worth comparing at this point the account given by Hippolytus of Rome[9] concerning a certain Alcibiades of Apamea in Syria who came to Rome with a book which he claimed that one Elchasai had got from Parthia (*Refutatio omnium haeresium*, 9.13.1). This text had originally been revealed by an angel of gigantic proportions, who was the Son of God, and was paired with a female angel called the Holy Spirit (cf. Epiphanius, *Panarion*, 19.4.1–2). (Hippolytus' account may draw on the preaching of Alcibiades, and the contents of the book of Elchasai, and his own knowledge of an Elchasaite group, and this may be the reason for some tensions in his account.) According to Hippolytus[10] obedience to the Jewish Law, including circumcision, was part of the Elchasaite message as propagated by Alcibiades in Rome (9.14.1). They also practised baptism, and indeed a second baptism if a baptized person had been sexually impure (9.15.1). The accompanying purifications included calling on seven 'witnesses', namely heaven, water, the holy spirits, the angels of prayer, oil, salt and the earth; 'these constitute the astonishing, ineffable and great mysteries of Elchasai which he reveals to

---

[7] E. Schweizer, 'Christ in the Letter to the Colossians', in *RevExp* 70 (1973), pp. 451–67, here p. 454.

[8] Reff. in, e.g., J. Gnilka, *Der Kolosserbrief*, HTKNT 10/1 (Freiburg, Herder, 1980), p. 122.

[9] Cf. A. F. J. Klijn and G. J. Reinink, *Patristic Evidence for Jewish–Christian Sects*, NovTSup 36 (Leiden, Brill, 1973), pp. 114–21. This account has many parallels with that which Epiphanius of Salamis gives of the 'Ossaeans' or 'Ossenes' (*Panarion*, 19.1.1–6.4 – Klijn–Reinink, pp. 154–61; note that they believe that Epiphanius' account is independent of Hippolytus – p. 63).

[10] Cf. Epiphanius, *Panarion*, 19.1.5; 19.5.1: Elxai 'did not live according to the Law', and the Ossenes 'rejected the books of Moses', yet they followed 'the Jewish way of life in observing the sabbath, circumcision and doing everything the Law prescribes'! (Cf. also Klijn–Reinink, *Patristic Evidence*, pp. 258–9.)

worthy pupils' (9.15.2; cf. 9.15.5).[11] At a later point Hippolytus mentions the Elchasaites using incantations and baptisms
'in their acceptance of the elements' or 'as they acknowledge
the elements' (10.29.3, *stoicheia* again), and the seven 'witnesses' may well therefore in this tradition be described as
*stoicheia*. Certain days are also significant because they are
under the influence of 'wicked stars of impiety' and no work is
started on them. The sabbath too is to be honoured in this way
(9.16.2–3), even if the avoidance of work on it is thereby given
a motivation worthy of Gnostic revaluations of Jewish
traditions.

Now at one point Hippolytus notes the similarities of these
Elchasaite teachings to those of the Pythagoreans, and indeed
claims that they were borrowed from them (9.4.1–2; cf. 9.17.2).
It is true that he has in mind the Pythagoreans' doctrine of
transmigration and their astrological skills, but it is apparent
that most of the parallels which could be detected between the
Pythagoreans and the background to the Letter to the Colossians could equally well be found in these accounts of Elchasaite teaching, and the latter shows even closer parallels in its
vision and its belief in angels and in its observance of the Jewish
Law, at least according to some accounts. The origins of these
Elchasaite traditions in the early second century,[12] are later
than the likely date of Colossians and lie further to the East, in
Parthia and Syria, but they were known in Rome too, and they
still show the sort of blend of idea and practice that could
conceivably have arisen anywhere where there were Jews or
Jewish Christians living in a pagan environment and seeking to
blend their traditions with those around them. To that extent
it may serve as an instructive parallel without our in any way
needing to suggest that precisely this group, or even one
derived from it, was present in Colossae.

[11] For Epiphanius there are two groups of seven witnesses, the first being 'salt, water,
earth, bread, heaven, air and wind', the second corresponding to Hippolytus' list –
*Panarion*, 19.1.5–6. *Panarion*, 30.17 lists eight which seem to be a fusion of elements of
both lists (cf. the synopsis in Klijn–Reinink, *Patristic Evidence*, pp. 57–8 n. 3).
[12] Cf. the often rather similar ones found in the Pseudo-Clementine literature (a body
of writings ostensibly by Clement, the first-century bishop of Rome, but probably
dating from fourth-century Syria although they contain earlier traditions).

In such a group a veneration of *stoicheia* in the sense of certain selected physical elements or 'constituent parts'[13] of the world may have been coupled with a Jewish linking of these elements with angelic powers and an observance of the Jewish Law or parts of it. For both the passages which we have considered suggest that it would be very misguided to distinguish too sharply between the two possible senses of *stoicheia* as physical elements and as powers, benign or malign, controlling human life. However, the way in which Paul treats service of the Jewish Law as service of the 'elements of the world' in Gal. 4.3, 9 should warn us that the opponents in Colossae need not have regarded their religion as a worship of the elements (or indeed as a 'worship of angels', 2.18) any more than Jews so regarded theirs, or any more than they regarded it as merely a matter of human traditions (2.8; cf. 2.22). In other words, this phrase, 'elements of the world', may be a polemical and contemptuous denigration of their beliefs like Jewish polemic against pagan cults as the worship of sticks and stones (cf. the contemptuous reference in Wis. 13.2). For a Greek would have interpreted the phrase, 'the elements of the world', primarily as a reference to the physical elements that make up the world, however much they may also have been regarded as exercising a quasi-personal influence on human life.[14] After all, Paul also takes the term 'flesh', *sarx*, that commonly denotes the physical stuff of the human body, and treats it as a quasi-personal power that exercises a baneful influence on our lives.[15] A similar polemic against the 'elements' and their influence should not then cause surprise, particularly in view of the widespread belief at that time that the course of human lives was dictated by heavenly bodies. As L. Hartman points out, the author of Colossians seems to share with the world of that time the belief that the 'cosmos ... was alive, filled and swayed by all sorts of

---

[13] So the argument of N. Kehl, *Der Christushymnus im Kolosserbrief: eine motivgeschichtliche Untersuchung zu Kol 1,15–20*, SBM 1 (Stuttgart, Katholisches Bibelwerk, 1967), ch. 6.

[14] Cf. Philo, *Vit. Mos.*, 1.96; 2.53; *Vit. cont.*, 3.

[15] Because of the Galatian opponents' stress on the physical rite of circumcision their version of Christianity can be contemptuously dismissed as a matter of 'flesh' as opposed to 'spirit' (Gal. 3.3). This is at least part of the reason for Paul's choice of the former term to characterize their position.

living powers', and he points out how even so sophisticated a Jew as Philo could treat the heavenly bodies, not as gods, it is true, but as God's lieutenants exercising power over the world.[16]

Such a background is the more plausible because the region of Phrygia (to which Colossae was reckoned to belong in the Roman period) possessed a considerable Jewish population. We do not hear specifically of Jews at Colossae, but the chances that there were some are high. One often reads, moreover, that the Jewish population of Phrygia were noted for their syncretistic beliefs and their blending of their traditions with those of surrounding paganism, yet the evidence for this is somewhat precarious.[17] If we want somewhat clearer, but by no means incontrovertible, evidence of Jews involving themselves more deeply in the life of their pagan environment, we must look slightly further afield: at Miletus on the coast there was a place in the theatre reserved for 'Jews who are also God-fearing' (*theosebioi*)[18] and in nearby Iasus we read of a certain Nicetas from Jerusalem, who *may* have been a Jew, contributing 100 drachmae to the festivals of Dionysus.[19] It is not impossible that some such spirit of give and take may have existed between Jews in Colossae and their neighbours and that it is to this blend of Jewish and non-Jewish religiosity that we owe the ideas against which the author of Colossians warns.

In such a setting it is easy to see how Diaspora Jews might partially assimilate their faith to the prevailing culture around

[16] 'Universal Reconciliation (Col. 1,20)', in *Studien zum Neuen Testament und seiner Umwelt*, 10 (1985), pp. 109–21, here p. 112, quoting Philo, *Spec. leg.*, 1.13–20.

[17] Cf. W. M. Ramsay, *The Cities and Bishoprics of Phrygia, Being an Essay of the Local History of Phrygia from the Earliest Times to the Turkish Conquest* (Oxford, Clarendon, 1897), p. 674. But there is no need for Julia Severa, who built a synagogue in Acmonia and who was also a high-priestess of the imperial cult, to have been a Jewess, despite Ramsay's assertion that it is 'obvious' that she was (p. 650). This *is* evidence, however, for influential patronage of the Jewish community there in the first century CE – cf. E. Schürer, *The History of the Jewish People in the Age of Jesus Christ*, vol. 3.1 (Edinburgh, Clark, 1986²), p. 31. Ramsay himself grants this argument here is 'a matter of speculation and uncertainty, where each step is more slippery than the preceding one' (ibid.); if his important first step is so uncertain perhaps we should not follow him down that path.

[18] *CII*, 748, second–third century CE. But cf. Schürer, *History*, p. 167, which inclines to the view that 'God-fearing' Gentiles may have been called 'Jews'.

[19] *CII*, 749, mid second century BCE.

them, identifying as angels the cosmic forces which their pagan neighbours believed controlled the world and their personal destinies.[20] The restrictions imposed upon them by the Jewish way of life could also be coupled with ascetic traditions found in contemporary paganism. These remain legal requirements, the *dogmata* of 2.14, commands to which one submits (*dogmatizesthe*, 2.20)[21] by obeying prohibitions on touching or drinking certain things. The focus would then not be on the Jewish Law as such, but on those of its commandments, perhaps with other, yet more rigorous ones added to them, which would form the basis for an ascetic way of life.[22] At the same time they are Jewish commandments, and F. Zeilinger may therefore be correct in seeing many of the statements of Colossians as seeking to outdo claims made for the Law, particularly in Jewish wisdom traditions, and to replace it with Christ.[23] It is also true that Col. 3.11 would have added point if the Colossian church were exposed to Judaizing pressures. Otherwise it is hard to see why this verse is included, especially when the Jew–Greek distinction of Gal. 3.28 is emphasized by the addition of that of circumcision–uncircumcision.

This sort of Judaism would then at first sight be somewhat different in character from that which motivated the opponents whom Paul encountered in Galatia. There Paul's opponents seemingly demanded obedience to the Jewish Law in a form in which that obedience had traditionally been interpreted, but here there beckons a form of Diaspora Judaism which indeed also maintains the external observances of

---

[20] E. Käsemann, art. 'Kolosserbrief', in *RGG*[3] (1959), vol. 3, p. 1728, poses the alternative, 'Are the powers honoured because they are considered dangerous or because they represent the heavenly "fullness"?', but these are not necessarily alternatives; it could be thought dangerous to neglect or ignore the heavenly 'fullness'.

[21] This verse strongly suggests that these regulations were linked to the *stoicheia*, for 'dying to' the latter entails that one should no longer let *dogmata* be imposed on one. The *dogmata* are in force because of the position accorded to the elements.

[22] An abstinence which goes beyond any requirements of the Law seems to have been characteristic of some Diaspora Judaism of the period – A. J. M. Wedderburn, *The Reasons for Romans*, Studies of the NT and Its World (Edinburgh, Clark, 1989), pp. 33–4.

[23] *Der Erstgeborene der Schöpfung: Untersuchungen zur Formalstruktur und Theologie des Kolosserbriefes* (Wien, Herder, 1974), pp. 92, 106–7 *et passim*.

Judaism, but sets them within a new, more mystical and speculative framework that owes much to the pagan world around, as well as perhaps to mystical traditions within Jewish thought.[24] Even in Galatians too we could more easily understand how Paul could with such apparent daring identify the service of the Law with his converts' pre-Christian service of the 'elements of the world', if indeed his opponents there linked the service of the Law to the angelic powers who had given the Law, powers which Paul slightingly treats as part of this world (Gal. 4.3, 9). In Gal. 3.19 Paul would then be revaluing the angels' role by treating it as a sign of the Law's inferiority rather than a reason to venerate it. If a difference between the opposition in Colossae and that in Galatia is to be sought, it should perhaps rather be found in the basis upon which those opponents presented their appeal: the indications are that in Galatia the opponents argued for the abiding validity of the Jewish Law, prescribed as binding on Christians by the Jerusalem church, whereas in Colossae appeal seems to have been made to visionary experience, however one translates the enigmatic words of Col. 2.18.[25]

What remains uncertain is whether the proponents of this teaching against which Colossians is written were Christians, putting forward their views as the true form of Christianity, as was the case in Galatia, or whether they existed outside the Christian community as a seductive alternative to it. Was their 'philosophy' one which presented a rival to Christ or one which accorded Christ a too subordinate place in it? Or the writer of Colossians may have regarded them as propounding a rival faith, but if Colossians was written early enough, before Christianity and Judaism had become clearly distinct from one

---

[24] An identification of the opponents in Col. which F. F. Bruce traces back to Calvin – 'Colossian Problems 3: The Colossian Heresy', in *BSac* 141 (1984), pp. 195–208, here p. 197. He himself suggestively compares Jewish mysticism (pp. 201–4).

[25] It is very hard to take 'what he has seen' as dependent on *embateuōn* as in the RSV or NEB; the accusative following this verb usually denotes a place. 'Things which he has seen when entering [where? heaven?]' must then qualify 'self-abasement and worship of angels' (cf. F. O. Francis in F. O. Francis and W. A. Meeks (eds.), *Conflict at Colossae*, SBLSBS 4 (Cambridge MA, Scholars, 1975), pp. 163–95). Paul's opponents in 2 Cor. 10–13 may well also have appealed to visionary experiences *if* we can infer that this was what drove Paul to recount his own vision in 12.1–4.

another, they could have regarded themselves as both Christians and Jews.

At any rate it is against such a position, preoccupied with the control exercised by heavenly forces over the individual's well-being and salvation, that Colossians develops its stress on the supremacy of Christ in whom all divine power rests (1.19; 2.9), 'in whom all the treasures of wisdom and knowledge are hidden' (2.3), and upon whom all such heavenly forces are ultimately dependent and to whom they are subject (1.16, 20; 2.10, 15). 'Only a cosmic Christ, who is at once the soul of the world and its Creator, could satisfy and overcome the religious concern of the Colossian syncretism.'[26] Not only that, but he has taken all those who are his with him to his heavenly throne, set above all such cosmic powers (2.12–13; 3.1), and they are filled with the fullness of his divine power (2.10). Over against their concern to keep in with or manipulate these forces by cultic and ascetic practices the letter stresses the forgiveness and redemption that has already been brought by Christ (1.14; 2.13–15),[27] as well as advocating its own, perhaps surprisingly conventional, rules for Christians' conduct.

### THE BACKGROUND TO THE AUTHOR'S THEOLOGY

It was mentioned above that the author of Colossians was probably not Paul himself; thus the cultural background of the author is that much more uncertain. Yet it is certain that the apostle played an important role in his or her thought, and thus Paul's teachings may be counted as one of the most important factors in the author's background. So, for instance, while the image of the Church as a body may stem ultimately from Graeco-Roman philosophy, and especially from the Stoic tradition, Colossians has derived it from Paul's development of

[26] M.-A. Wagenführer, *Die Bedeutung Christi für Welt und Kirche: Studien zum Kolosser- und Epheserbrief* (Leipzig, Wigand, 1941), p. 19, quoted by E. Käsemann, 'A Primitive Christian Baptismal Liturgy', in *Essays on New Testament Themes*, SBT 41 (London, SCM, 1964), pp. 149–68, here p. 167.

[27] H. Weiss, 'The Law in the Epistle to the Colossians', in *CBQ* 34 (1972), pp. 294–314, here p. 309, pertinently asks whether 'forgiveness' was not something missing from the horizons of those whom the letter opposes.

this tradition in which the body is qualified as that of Christ (e.g. 1 Cor. 12.27).

However, there are other materials and traditions which the author employs, and the nature of these tends to confirm the conclusions reached in the previous section concerning those whose ideas the author of Colossians rejects. To that extent H. Merklein may be correct in describing Colossians, not as, strictly speaking, an interpretation of Pauline theology, but as 'a Pauline or Paulinizing interpretation of basic ideas which do not stem directly from Paul'.[28] For, if the likely source of those views was to be found in a Diaspora Judaism strongly influenced by, and open to, its pagan neighbours or in a Jewish Christianity that had itself emerged within such a Judaism, then it is understandable that the author of Colossians should draw upon that same thought-world for the materials for his or her response, even if that material had to be adapted or modified to a greater or lesser degree to make it serve the author's purpose. That would at least ensure that the author and his or her readers were talking a common language. But it is all the more natural and appropriate if the author's own world is that of such a Diaspora Judaism. That would be true if Paul himself were the author, but also perhaps even more true if the author was one of his fellow-workers like Timothy. At any rate, we can detect a more pronouncedly Greek point of view in 3.11 compared with Gal. 3.28 and 1 Cor. 12.13, with the addition of 'barbarians and Scythians' to the list of divisions transcended in Christ.

At any rate, just such a background has plausibly been suggested for at least two important parts of the letter, the Christological 'hymn'[29] found in 1.15–20 and the *Haustafel* or 'domestic code' found in 3.18–4.1.

---

[28] 'Paulinische Theologie in der Rezeption des Kolosser- und Epheserbriefes', in Merklein, *Studien zu Paulus und Jesus*, WUNT 43 (Tübingen, Mohr, 1987), pp. 409–53, here p. 422 (cf. p. 447).

[29] For the sake of convenience the term 'hymn' is used to refer to this passage, but cf. the doubts expressed by W. Schenk, 'Christus, das Geheimnis der Welt, als dogmatisches und ethisches Grundprinzip des Kolosserbriefes', in *EvT* 43 (1983), pp. 138–55, here pp. 144–6. I am more confident that something is quoted here, whatever its original form, context and scope.

With regard to the first of these passages there is widespread agreement that the author of Colossians has quoted a hymnic or credal passage, although this has been questioned. But there is less agreement as to the extent of the original form of this 'hymn'. However, a glance at the form of the passage as set out in fig. 1 shows two things:

(a) There are similarities in language between 1.15 and 1.18*b* and between 1.16 and 1.19–20. This lends support to the argument that the passage is a hymnic one, with either two strophes, 1.15–18*a* and 1.18*b*–20, or three, 1.15–16, 1.17–18*a* and 1.18*b*–20.[30]

(b) But at the same time it is apparent that even if the passage is divided into three the strophes are very ill-proportioned in relation to one another; that in turn lends credibility to the suggestion that an original 'hymn' has been expanded.

15*a* **who is** the image of the invisible God,

 *b* **the first-born** of all creation,

16*a* **for in him all** things were created,

 *b* **in heaven** and **on earth**,

 *c* visible and invisible,

 *d* (whether thrones or dominions

 *e* or principalities or authorities);

 *f* **all things** were created **through him** and **for him**;

18*b* **who is** the beginning,

 *c* **the first-born** from the dead,

 *d* that in everything he might be pre-eminent,

19 **for in him all** the fullness was pleased to dwell

20*a* and **through him** and **for him** to reconcile **all things**,

 *b* making peace (through the blood of his cross)

 *c* [through him], whether things **on earth** or

---

[30] For a brief listing of proponents of these and other divisions of the passage see J.-N. Aletti, *Colossiens 1,15–20: genre et exégèse du texte; fonction de la thématique sapientielle*, AnBib 91 (Rome, Biblical Inst., 1981), pp. 21–4.

17a  and he is before all     things **in heaven.**
     [things]
  b  and in him all things
     hold together,
18a  and he is the head of the
     body (the Church);

Fig. 1

There is a considerable measure of agreement about some of
these likely expansions, less about others;[31] the principal areas
of discussion are these:
(1) It seems odd that the list of 16*de* does not continue the
previous 'both ... and ...' structure, and seems to be an
elaboration only of the heavenly and invisible side of
things.[32] On the other hand, if the Colossians were
unhealthily preoccupied with heavenly powers, an addition that listed such powers which were dependent upon
Christ for their very existence would be both intelligible
and appropriate.[33] For it is not 'all things' that are a

---

[31] Cf. the lists in P. Benoit, 'L'hymne christologique de Col. 1,15–20: jugement critique
sur l'état de recherches', in *Christianity, Judaism and Other Greco-Roman Cults: Studies for
Morton Smith at Sixty*, SJLA 12, ed. J. Neusner (Leiden, Brill, 1975) vol. 1,
pp. 226–63, here p. 238 (table); C. Burger, *Schöpfung und Versöhnung: Studien zum
liturgischen Gut im Kolosser- und Epheserbrief*, WMANT 46 (Neukirchen-Vluyn,
Neukirchener, 1975), esp. pp. 9–11, 15–16; Gnilka, *Kol.* (n. 8), pp. 53–4.

[32] Assuming that this list does not contain both heavenly and earthly powers – see J. L.
Houlden, *Paul's Letters from Prison (Philippians, Colossians, Philemon and Ephesians)*,
Pelican NT Comms (Harmondsworth, Penguin, 1970), pp. 161, 163, following
E. Bammel, 'Versuch zu Kol 1¹⁵⁻²⁰', in *ZNW* 52 (1961), pp. 88–95. Yet it seems
arbitrary to pair these various terms in this way; contrast the (equally arbitrary?)
proposal of S. M. Baugh, 'The Poetic Form of Col. 1:15–20', in *WTJ* 47 (1985),
pp. 227–44, here 236, 240. W. Wink, *Naming the Powers: the Language of Power in the
New Testament* (Philadelphia, Fortress, 1984), pp. 11, 64–7, seeks to make all four
terms refer to both heavenly and earthly powers, but it would be reasonable to argue
that the interest here lies in the heavenly powers, just as he argues that the focus in
Rom. 13.1–7 is primarily on the earthly (pp. 45–7); it is true that the manifestations
of these powers may be earthly, but the point is that they are spoken of *as if* part of
another, invisible world.

[33] Cf. J. M. Robinson, 'A Formal Analysis of Col. 1:15–20', in *JBL* 76 (1957),
pp. 270–87, here p. 283; however, the point made by Kehl, *Christushymnus* (n. 13),
p. 34, is worth noting: if a Stoic triadic formula like that reflected in Rom. 11.36 lies
behind the 'in him ... through him ... for him' of 16*a* and 16*f*, then does this mean
that *at some stage* 16*bc* was inserted as well? But 20*c* seems to correspond to 16*b*.

problem for the letter; animals, plants, etc., are not an issue, but rather heavenly powers and people who fear them and venerate them.

(2) There is wide agreement that the phrase '(of) the Church' in verse 18a is an addition. For hitherto the passage has spoken of creation in general, and the relation of the one spoken of to 'all things' (neuter). There has been nothing to prepare for such a reference to the Church, and the consequent concentration on a group of human beings.

(3) The flow of thought of 1.18b–20a would suggest that the reconciliation of verse 20a was achieved by being the 'first-born from the dead', i.e. by resurrection. Yet verse 20b goes on to speak of a making peace through the blood of the cross, the cross which is the focus of attention in 2.14–15.

(4) Verse 20 presents a number of syntactical and textual problems: (a) 'having made peace' can hardly govern 'whether things on earth or things in heaven' as a direct object.[34] If both are allowed to remain, then the latter must be allowed to be in apposition to the 'all things' of 20a. (b) Some MSS, including some significant ones, include a second 'through him', in 20c. Some retain this, but, if retained, it must go with 'having made peace'. In that case 'through the blood of his cross' surely cannot also qualify 'having made peace'. So does that mean that 'through the blood of his cross' was added later (by the author of Colossians?) without removing the second 'through him', and that it was only later that scribes felt the awkwardness of the two 'through' phrases?

If that is the case then we are left with a text that looks like that of fig. 1 once the passages in round brackets are removed. But what would be the provenance of such a passage? It is hard to regard a hymn that includes verses 18b–20, with their clear reference to the resurrection, as being anything but a Christian composition, nor is it likely to be Gnostic.[35] Equally, however,

---

[34] Contrast, e.g., Prov. 10.10 LXX.
[35] On Gnostic discomfort with the idea of resurrection cf. Wedderburn, *Baptism* (n. 3), pp. 18–21, 212–18.

once the qualification '(of) the Church' is removed in verse
18*a*, the language of these verses, including the 'head–body'
relationship, seems to be being applied to the relationship
between the subject of verses 15–18*a* and the entire cosmos,
animate and inanimate. Such language would be unusual if
applied to Christ, but at least partial parallels in Graeco-
Roman thought suggest that similar language could there be
applied to God. That is certainly how the Jewish writer Aristo-
bulus (second century BCE) interpreted an Orphic poem which
he cited concerning Zeus's relation to the cosmos, as its 'beginning, middle and end', and whose sentiments he endorsed.[36]
However, the version he cites does not include the 'head–body'
image, but the reference to the 'head' is found in other versions
of this poem.[37] As early as Plato we also find the cosmos as a
body permeated and ruled by a divine soul,[38] and Greek
philosophy knew of God as the source of all things who holds
them together.[39] The idea of cosmic reconciliation is harder to
parallel, but E. Schweizer has argued that this passage in
Colossians presupposes a scenario of cosmic strife such as is
found in Graeco-Roman thought of the period,[40] or, as
E. Schillebeeckx puts it,[41] the people of this region 'were aware
of a cosmic fault, a kind of catastrophe in the universe, a gulf
between the higher (heavenly) and the lower (earthly) world.

---

[36] In Eusebius, *Praep. ev.*, 13.12.4–8; ET in *OTP*, vol. 2, 840–1. A large number of
poems circulated at that time under the name of the legendary bard Orpheus.

[37] In Ps.-Aristotle, *De mundo*, 7.401*a*29 we find Zeus as 'head' from whom all things
have been created, yet without the answering image of the body (= O. Kern,
*Orphicorum fragmenta* (Berlin, Weidmann, 1922), no. 21*a*; cf. 168; also in col. 13 line
12 of the Derveni papyrus (fourth century BCE): R. Merkelbach, 'Der orphische
Papyrus von Derveni', in *Zeitschrift für Papyrologie und Epigraphie*, 1 (1967),
pp. 21–32, here p. 23; also app. to vol. 47 (1982), p. 8). On the cosmic body of God
cf. *PGM*, 12.243; 13.767–72; 21.3–7 (heaven is the head).

[38] Cf. e.g. Plato, *Tim.*, 34A–C (yet for Plato the visible cosmos is God's image – 92c);
further E. Schweizer in *TDNT*, vol. 7, pp. 1029–30, 1037–8.

[39] Cf. Ps.-Aristotle, *De mundo*, 6.397*b*14–15: 'all things are from God and are constituted (*synestēken*) for us by God' (tr. D. J. Furley, LCL; cf. Kern, *Orph. fr.*, 168.7).

[40] Esp. 'Slaves of the Elements and Worshippers of Angels: Gal. 4:3, 9 and Col. 2:8, 18,
20', in *JBL* 107 (1988), pp. 455–68, and 'Versöhnung des Alls (Kolosser 1,20)', in
Schweizer, *Neues Testament und Christologie im Werden: Aufsätze* (Göttingen, Vandenhoeck & Ruprecht, 1982), pp. 164–78, but also 'Colossians 1:15–20', in *Rev Exp*, 87
(1990), pp. 97–104.

[41] *Christ: the Christian Experience in the Modern World* (London, SCM, 1980), p. 182; cf.
p. 191.

The problem of meaning and meaninglessness is experienced in cosmic terms and is expressed in a longing for salvation which will consist in the restoration of the unity of the cosmos.' Whether the breach is one between heaven and earth, or between the warring elements that make up the entire cosmos, as in the texts which Schweizer cites, some such cosmic dislocation and disruption of the harmony of the creation, created in, and held together by, the one mediator, seems to be presupposed here.

However, what pagans asserted of God, Hellenistic Jews generally preferred to assert of a power or personified aspect of God, like the divine *logos* ('word', 'reason') or wisdom. Wisdom was described as God's image,[42] and so too is the *logos*.[43] This wisdom or *logos* could be described as God's 'first-born' (*prōtogonos*),[44] as the 'beginning' of God's ways (Prov. 8.22), as holding all things together (Sir. 43.26).[45] Philo, too, uses the idea of the *logos* as head of the body that is the world of the incorporeal *logoi* or souls.[46] In this respect Philo would come nearer to the thought behind Col. 1.18a than any other Graeco-Roman parallels.[47] However, it is of God that Philo

---

[42] Wis. 7.26; Philo, *Leg. all.*, 1. 43.

[43] Philo, *Conf. ling.*, 147; *Rer. div. her.*, 231; *Som.*, 1.239; *Spec. leg.*, 1.81; cf. *Op.mund.*, 25.

[44] Philo, *Agric.*, 51; *Conf. ling.*, 146; *Som.*, 1.215. J. Fossum, 'Colossians 1.15–18a in the Light of Jewish Mysticism and Gnosticism', in *NTS*, 35 (1989), pp. 183–201, here p. 190, also compares Orig., *Comm. on John*, 2.31, where a fragment of the *Prayer of Joseph* has Jacob describe himself as '*prōtogonos* of every living creature' as well as 'archangel of the power of the Lord' (*OTP*, vol. 2, p. 713; cf. pp. 703–4).

[45] A different term is used here from that of Col. 1.17. The *logos* is also the bond of all things, holding all together, according to Philo (*Fug.*, 112; cf. *Quaest. in Exod.*, 2.118. It is interesting to compare here the role of Zeus's reason, *phronēsis*, in col. 15 of the Derveni papyrus: Merkelbach, 'Papyrus' (n. 37), pp. 24–5.

[46] *Som.*, 1.128. An even clearer parallel would be found in *Quaest. in Exod.*, 2.117 if we could be sure that this was not a Christian interpolation: 'The head of all things is the eternal *logos* of the eternal God, under which, as if it were his feet or other limbs, is placed the whole world, over which he passes and firmly stands' (tr. R. Marcus, LCL, who brackets this entire passage, which goes on to speak of Christ; moreover, it interrupts the discussion of the high priest's garments).

[47] If, however, it should be argued that none of these parallels come near enough to provide the background for a cosmic body of which the head is wisdom or Christ then, rather than holding '(of) the Church' to be an original part of the 'hymn' (introducing the second half?), it may be simpler to regard the whole of verse 18a as an insertion into an originally cosmic context, or else to retain 'and he is the head' (ventured by Kehl, *Christushymnus* (n. 13), p. 98) as in the Orphic hymn quoted above.

speaks when he speaks of God who 'destroys faction (*staseis*) . . . in the various parts of the universe'; for 'nature is at strife in herself, when her parts make onslaught one on another and her law-abiding sense of equality is vanquished by the greed for inequality' (he is thinking of natural calamities like droughts).[48] Yet the *logos* is given the role of announcing his peace[49] and of mediating between the various elements of the universe[50] and controlling them.[51] Finally, we should note that when the seer of Revelation writes to the church at Laodicea, near Colossae, Christ speaks as one who is the 'beginning of God's creation' (Rev. 3.14), again using language and ideas which are very much at home in Hellenistic Jewish speculation on wisdom and the divine *logos*. That perhaps suggests that such ideas were current in that area and could appropriately be used in addressing Christians there. Furthermore, other passages in the New Testament which also show signs of a similar cosmic Christology also bear the marks of the influence of Hellenistic Jewish speculations of this sort (e.g. Heb. 1.2–3).

It is therefore possible that the first part of this passage may already have existed in a Jewish form, as a statement about the relationship of God or more likely the divine *logos* or wisdom to creation, although it should be noted that neither term occurs in the Colossian 'hymn'. In that case we would have to reckon with possibly three or more levels in this passage, at least three stages in its formation: (a) an original statement or statements (not necessarily yet in hymnic form) by Hellenistic Jews about the relationship of God to the creation, which were then (b) applied by Hellenistic Jewish Christians to Christ by adding most of verses 18*b*–20, and by other insertions, and finally (c) adopted and adapted by the writer of Colossians for the particular polemical context of the letter (verse 16*de*?). However, it must to some extent remain uncertain what was added at what stage. The addition of '(of) the Church' in 18*a*, for instance, might have been regarded as belonging to the last

[48] *Spec. leg.*, 2.190–2; ?cf. *Quaest. in Gen.*, 3.7.
[49] *Rer. div. her.*, 206.
[50] *Plant.*, 10.
[51] *Agric.*, 51; on these and other reff. cf. Hartman, 'Reconciliation' (n. 16), pp. 115–18.

stage, were it not for the statement in 2.10 that Christ is 'head
over every principality and authority', which gives the headship of Christ a wider scope than just the Church. (It would be
unwise to distinguish the figurative 'headship over' too sharply
from the physiological imagery of the 'head–body' contrast.
The author seems to slide from one to the other without being
aware that these are two different senses of 'head', any more
than Paul is in 1 Cor. 11.3–5.) Equally, however, 2.19 can be
seen as elaborating the imagery of verse 18a. So the author
seems able happily to make use of both ideas, the 'body' as the
cosmos, including its powers, and the 'body' as the Church,
even if their relation one to another is somewhat ill-defined.
That should make us cautious of regarding one as correcting
the other. It suggests rather that the author regarded the two
as complementary and was prepared to use both, whether or
not '(of) the Church' was his or her own addition to the
tradition.

With regard to the provenance of the other suggested major
piece of traditional material in the letter, the 'domestic code' of
3.18–4.1, J. E. Crouch has argued that the 'code' found in
Colossians, with its emphasis on the mutual responsibility to
one another of wives and husbands, children and fathers, slaves
and their owners, does not stem directly from Stoic thought as
some earlier scholars supposed, but indirectly *via* Hellenistic
Judaism. However, it was not so much 'borrowed' from this
source by Christians as converted to the service of Christ along
with the rest of the intellectual heritage of those Hellenistic
Jews who espoused the new faith.[52] A derivation ultimately
from Greek philosophical thought, perhaps mediated by Hellenistic Judaism, is still maintained, but with important modifications, by D. Lührmann and others:[53] this material derives

---

[52] Esp. *The Origin and Intention of the Colossian Haustafel* (Göttingen, Vandenhoeck &
Ruprecht, 1972), p. 149.
[53] 'Wo man nicht mehr Sklave oder Freier ist: 'Überlegungen zur Struktur frühchri-
stlicher Gemeinden', in *WD*, 13 (1975), pp. 53–83, esp. pp. 75–9, and 'Neutestamentliche Haustafeln und antike Oikonomie', in *NTS*, 27 (1980–1), pp. 83–97. (He
wishes to limit the 'Stoic list of duties' to a definition of the general relationships of
the 'wise' as in Epict., *Diss.* 2.17.31.) Cf. further D. L. Balch, 'Household Codes', in
*Greco-Roman Literature and the New Testament*, ed. D. E. Aune, SBLSBS 21 (Atlanta,
Scholars, 1988), pp. 25–50, esp. pp. 26–8, 48–50 (bibliography); he claims that
there is now a general consensus as to this derivation (35).

not so much from what Crouch describes as 'the Stoic list of duties' (*ta kathēkonta*) as from a tradition designated as *oikonomia* or *ho oikonomikos*, that is, that branch of philosophy relating to the management of the household. Whether it is right to describe this as a quite different tradition from the 'list of duties' is not clear, since Seneca, *Ep.*, 94.1, which he cites, gives the advice offered on the treatment of one's wives, children and slaves as an example of that sort of philosophy which is not concerned with humanity in general, but rather prescribes the duties appropriate to each person (in their respective positions in life). The list of duties appropriate within a household would then be a subdivision within this branch of ethics. This tradition too was known to a Hellenized Jew like Philo as a branch of ethics, the art of improving human conduct which the wise person possesses (esp. *Ebr.*, 91–2), even if he did not make use of the material in it in quite that form which is relevant here, the threefold list of mutual responsibilities. Thus it is possible that this tradition too came into Christian use *via* Hellenistic Judaism.[54] That such a tradition was adopted by Christians is only too understandable in view of the importance of the household as the focus of early Christian life and worship. However, it is important to note that the tradition needed to be adapted. So Lars Hartman argues both that a passage like Col. 3.18–4.1 owes more to the Graeco-Roman world for its contents, the attitudes and social conventions which it reflects, than for its literary form (there is no evidence of a literary form of 'household code' lying ready to hand for early Christians to use), and that a feature like the element of reciprocity was incorporated because it was felt to be 'apt', 'in the Lord'.[55]

Thus we may infer that both the author of Colossians and his or her readers were at home in the world of a Diaspora Judaism that showed a considerable awareness of, and openness to, the

---

[54] The same provenance is also quite likely for the lists of vices and virtues in 3.5, 8–9, 12 if S. Schulz is right in seeing them as dependent on the Decalogue, the OT moral code and the 'Hellenistic Jewish tradition of ethical instruction' (*Neutestamentliche Ethik*, Zürcher Grundrisse zur Bibel (Zürich, TVZ, 1987), pp. 560–1, 564–5); see also ch. 2 n. 68.

[55] 'Some Unorthodox Thoughts on the "Household-Code" Form', in *The Social World of Formative Christianity and Judaism: Essays in Tribute to Howard Clark Kee*, ed. J. Neusner *et al.* (Philadelphia, Fortress, 1988), pp. 219–32.

ideas of the Graeco-Roman world around them. Neither as Jews nor as Christians were they slow in appropriating what they could of the cultural world in which they lived, pressing it into the service first of the Jewish faith and then of Christ. However, it is the risk in all such borrowings that the borrowed material does not fit altogether comfortably into its new context (Mark 2.21–2 parr.!) and the thought of Colossians is witness to the sort of tensions and strains that such adaptations provoke.

# CHAPTER 2

# The theology of Colossians

The chief focus of theological interest in Colossians is the hymn of 1.15–20 and the use which the author of the letter makes of it, for it contains ideas and claims for the status and work of Christ which are to some extent unparalleled in the New Testament. That in turn raises a hermeneutical problem which will also concern us in chapter 4: once one recognizes a difference, at least of emphasis, between the author and the hymn, does one interpret the hymn in its own right or only as the author of Colossians utilizes it? For this is a text that is part of a canon to which a religious community, the Christian Church, looks at least for guidance (or which serves as an authoritative norm for some). To whom are they to listen, only to the witness to Christ of the author of the letter or also to the at least differently nuanced witness borne by those whom the writer quotes?

Yet there is more to Colossians than just the hymn and its interpretation and application to the situation in Colossae, and so this chapter looks also at two other important features of the letter, its 'realized eschatology' which seems to reflect a marked development of Pauline theology, and the relationship between its theology and its ethical teaching, a relationship which is basically Pauline in structure, even if the ethical teaching which flows from it bears distinctive marks of Graeco-Roman culture and of the thought-world of the hymn, features which distinguish it in certain respects from the ethical teaching of the letters agreed to be by Paul.

23

## THE CHRISTOLOGICAL HYMN (1.15–20)

In the first chapter it was argued that this passage quotes a hymn or creed which was based upon Hellenistic Jewish speculations about God's wisdom or *logos*, but which has taken on a clearly Christian form thanks to the inclusion of a strophe which speaks of the cosmic role of the risen Christ. The adoption of such Jewish material clearly has far-reaching implications for the development of Christological thought, for language originally applied to what may at times have been little more than an oblique reference to God, or a personification of a divine attribute or power, is now applied to the historical figure of an individual human being, Jesus of Nazareth. At the same time, the source of such ideas, in Hellenistic Jewish speculations about the role of wisdom or the *logos* in creation, needs to be carefully noted, in view of the fact that 'Theodore's interpretation of Col. 1:15–17 in terms of a new creation instead of the first creation has taken on crucial importance even in commentaries of medieval and modern times'.[1] The background of the ideas used in this passage therefore suggests that, however much this is said of Christ who is also the first-fruits of a new creation, it is yet a role in relation to the original creation which is being claimed for him.

The assertion that Christ was God's image (1.15) is in itself not so problematic, for it could be held that any human being was God's image, although in 1 Cor. 11.7 Paul limited this dignity to males; in 2 Cor. 4.4 he expressly describes Christ as God's image. Two verses later, however, his language seems to reflect the creation story of Gen. 1, so the claim of verse 4 may be a stronger one: this image of God is not just any person, but the original pattern according to which all people are created. Paul, however, elsewhere describes this pattern as manifested only in the end-time: he contrasts with the original human creation that of the end-time when Christ 'the last (*eschatos*) Adam' is manifested (1 Cor. 15.45). Now Colossians seems to be asserting that this pattern, this model, already existed at the

---

[1] Schweizer, *Col.* (ch. 1 n. 5), p. 263; cf. 250–1 (the ref. is to Theodore of Mopsuestia, fourth–fifth centuries).

beginning, not in a concrete human being, but in a form analogous to that of the divine wisdom or *logos*. Yet, at the same time, the qualification 'of the invisible God' recalls John 1.18 and its assertion that, although no one has seen God, the Son, coming from the Father, has made God known. That suggests that the reference here is to one who indeed gives concrete, incarnate expression to the invisible divine nature. The problem is how one who was only manifested later played this role in creation. Can this be resolved without falling into some of the tangles that beset later Christology (e.g. distinguishing the eternal *logos* from the person in whom it was incarnate)?

The protological reference is at any rate clear when Colossians continues 'first-born of all creation'. What is less clear is whether this phrase means 'born first before all creation' or 'born first before (all the rest of) creation', which would imply that Christ was part of creation. Now in the case of wisdom in Prov 8.22ff. there is room for doubt, for God creates (*ektisen*) wisdom,[2] and yet does so before anything else is formed. However, the distinction of 'begotten not made' that was to be so important in later creeds was, as far as we know, not yet a concern of Christians at this early stage, and they evidently were still happy to apply such a phrase to Christ. They sought thereby to stress Christ's pre-eminence *vis-à-vis* God's creation and his sovereignty over it. In their use of language here they were not so much interested in the relationship between Christ and God. As Calvin puts it, 'what is here treated of is, not what He is in Himself, but what He accomplishes in others'.[3]

This relationship between Christ and creation, all of it, is

---

[2] Cf. Sir. 24.9. J. D. G. Dunn, *Christology in the Making: a New Testament Inquiry into the Origins of the Doctrine of the Incarnation* (London, SCM, 1980), p. 189, notes a 'similar ambivalence' in later stages of the wisdom tradition. Modern physics may push us beyond this issue: does it make sense to speak at all of time 'before creation'? Does time exist without creation? Cf., e.g., P. Davies, *God and the New Physics* (Harmondsworth, Penguin, 1984), p. 38, aptly quoting Augustine (cf. *De civitate Dei*, 11.5–6: 'there is no time before the cosmos'; 'the cosmos was created, not in time, but together with time'; also *Confessions*, 11.13). The point was already made by Philo in the first century: *Op.mund.* 26; cf. *Leg. all.* 1.2.

[3] *The Epistles of Paul the Apostle to the Galatians, Ephesians, Philippians and Colossians*, tr. T. H. L. Parker (Edinburgh/London, Oliver & Boyd, 1965), p. 309.

expounded further in Col. 1.16: all things were created 'in
him', 'through him' and 'for him'. The first of these phrases
should perhaps not be taken locally or spatially, but rather in
an instrumental sense[4] or, possibly better, since it avoids
making the following 'through him' redundant, as a phrase
expressing the manner, the pattern of, or model for, the creation of all things:[5] all things were created according to him,
with reference to him.[6]

As we have seen, the hymn, in the form in which it now
exists, elaborates at some length on the 'all things', listing in all
probability a variety of alternative terms for unseen heavenly
powers. Even these were created by God with reference to
Christ. They too were created 'through him' as God's agent in
creation, and 'for him'. That Christ was the purpose or goal
with reference to which all things were created is, as Schweizer
notes,[7] harder to explain purely from the thought-world of
Hellenistic Judaism than are the other two phrases used here.
In Rom. 11.36 (which uses precisely the same trio of preposi-
tions as here)[8] and 1 Cor. 8.6 Paul speaks of *God* as the purpose
for which all things or all of us exist, using the same preposition
as found here, *eis*.[9] In all likelihood this preposition has in the
usage of both Paul and of Colossians an eschatological orienta-
tion that is not usually found in either Jewish wisdom speculation or in the Stoic terminology that is often quoted as a
parallel.[10] However, when we ask how Christ might be viewed

[4] Kehl, *Christushymnus* (ch. 1 n. 13), p. 106, compares Ps. 103.24 LXX; Wis. 9.1.
[5] Gnilka, *Kol.* (ch. 1 n. 8), p. 64, citing also Kehl and A. Feuillet, describes this as a
relational or exemplary use of *en*. Burger, *Schöpfung* (ch. 1 n. 31), p. 44, who does not
include 'through him', etc., in the original hymn, yet distinguishes the role expressed
by *en* here by describing it as passive, rather than active, and elsewhere speaks of
Christ as the 'model' for creation.
[6] Shading over into the use of *en* expressing relation or respect – cf. A. J. M.
Wedderburn, 'Some Observations on Paul's Use of the Phrases "in Christ" and
"with Christ"', in *JSNT* 25 (1985), pp. 83–97, here p. 85 with the *caveat* on p. 86.
[7] *Col.* (ch. 1 n. 5), p. 70. Cf. the rabbinic view that the world was created 'for the sake
of the Messiah' (*b. Sanh.* 98*b*).
[8] Cf. M. Aur. 4.23.
[9] The same preposition is found reasonably frequently in the LXX, esp. in Sir., with
the verb 'create', but not followed by a person or personification as the purpose
of creation.
[10] That can be seen from the rather different sense that this preposition often seems to
have in these parallels, as quoted, e.g., in E. Lohse, *Colossians and Philemon*,

as the purpose or goal of creation, then it is difficult not to see this as anticipating the role of Christ as expressed in verses 18*b*–20, that is as the risen one who restores creation to what it was intended to be (but had perhaps never been, although the author never expressly discloses whether he or she believed in a state of primal innocence before the fall). That in turn is foreshadowed by the idea in Rom. 8.20–1 of a creation waiting in hope for liberation, a liberation, however, that is linked with the glory of God's children (plural) rather than as here with the single figure of the one who is God's image.

Yet how can we meaningfully speak of the Christ who was Jesus of Nazareth playing a role in the creation of the world? Is this not simply a case of an incongruous mythological frame-work being imposed upon that historical figure by early Christians in a way which they hoped would be meaningful to their contemporaries, but which is nonsense to our age? Or is this language 'simply ... the writer's way of saying that Christ now reveals the character of the power behind the world'?[11] But, while that conviction may be at least partly what led Christians to make this claim, the claim itself actually seems to go further and to ascribe a role in creation to Jesus Christ. The hymn emphatically speaks of him, and not so much of God. Or can we say that, if humanity can be spoken of as the goal, the highest life-form, of creation, and if Jesus can be thought of as being essentially what that humanity was meant to be, then this comes near to expressing the convictions which led those early Christians to this conclusion? Yet such a view ascribes to the ordering of our world and the evolution of its life-forms a purposiveness and a providential arrangement which not all would be prepared to grant, even if the alternative is the perhaps equally startling claim that all is in the last analysis a coincidence, a fortuitous happening. Moreover, Dunn is surely correct to see a background in wisdom speculation rather than

Hermeneia (Philadelphia, Fortress, 1971; ET of MeyerK 9/2 (Göttingen, Vanden-hoeck & Ruprecht, 1968[14]), pp. 51–2 n. 137; see also Philo, *Spec. leg.*, 1.208. It may also explain why a different preposition, *dia* with the accus., is used by Philo when he speaks of the 'final cause' of something in Aristotelian terms (*Cher.*, 125–8; *Prov.*, 1.23; *Quaest. in Gen.*, 1.58).

[11] Dunn, *Christology* (n. 2), p. 190.

in that concerning Christ as the 'last Adam'.[12] In that case such an anthropological interpretation of the hymn involves a considerable reinterpretation, for the first strophe does not appear to be speaking of Christ as a human being but as a divine being. Although there are those, Dunn himself included, who see the first strophe as referring already to the exalted human being of the second strophe, this does not seem to do justice to the original hymn. It only becomes more plausible if the reference to 'the Church' in 1.18a is part of the original text; however we have seen the problems which that presents in understanding 1.15–18a as a whole. So, if we cannot say that the hymn originally spoke of Jesus as an archetypal human being, but of the divine Christ, we today will have to express in very different terms our convictions about the relation to creation of that Jesus whom we call Christ. However, a good starting-point will be to recognize that a *Christian* view of God must be able to portray a God of creation who is still recognizably the same as the God to whom Jesus pointed us and in whose name and as whose representative he spoke and acted.

That Christ is or exists 'before all' (1.17a) can be understood either temporally or with reference to rank or as both at once; in the case of the first of these the present tense is surprising, unless there is a possible allusion to the divine name as in John 8.58, 'Before Abraham was, I *am*'; yet this is by far the commoner sense of the preposition and is to be preferred. The pre-eminence of Christ is expressed more directly by verse 18d.

We have seen that the assertion that all is held together in Christ (verse 17b) is closely paralleled in Sirach by an assertion about God's *logos* (43.26) and by Philo's view that the divine *logos* was the bond holding all together. The idea is now used here to give expression to Christ's continuing role in the sustaining of creation as opposed to merely helping to bring it into being. Given the background of the hymn in Hellenistic Jewish speculation about God's wisdom or *logos*, one can see the logic which brought early Christians to make this claim for Christ, but it is at first sight hard to see how such claims can meaning-

[12] Ibid. p. 188.

fully be made today for a human individual, however much we reinterpret these mythological claims. One can then readily see the attractions of the view of Theodore of Mopsuestia, noted above, that 1.15–17 described the role of Christ in a new creation, not the original one. For, if we were to regard him as the representative of the humanity of the new age, we could perhaps at least glimpse how, in a situation in which humanity has in its power to destroy this little corner of the cosmos in which it lives, a pattern of human existence that sets its face against those forces that could destroy that world, that bit of cosmos, could be said to sustain and preserve that world. Yet, with a vastly widened view of the universe, we must grant that even this claim in no way matches up to the range of this statement in Colossians; still less does it do justice to the claims seemingly made on behalf of Christ's role in the original creation of the world. For we have already seen that the background of such statements does not seem to be primarily a discussion of Christ's role as a human being, the Adam of the end-time, but rather draws on affirmations about Christ as God's wisdom or *logos*.

In 18a, as we have seen, a Christian hand has probably taken the cosmological imagery of wisdom or the *logos* as head of the body, the cosmos, or as head of the cosmos, and has applied it to Christ, but that hand or another has then introduced the qualification that the head's 'body' is the Church, in other words just a part of the cosmos, and indeed just a part of the humanity that is in the cosmos. (The scope of Christ's headship is thus limited in much the same way as I have just suggested his sustaining of all things needs to be limited in its scope to be intelligible.) There has been little to prepare us for this qualification, and it could thus seem to be a gratuitous and alien intrusion. Yet we can see in Rom. 8.19–24 how the Church, the redeemed people, is in its way the trail-blazer for the whole of inanimate creation, for, if in its groans of distress 'unredeemed mankind is spokesman for his world',[13] then redeemed humanity leads the way into God's freedom for both

---

[13] E. Käsemann, *Commentary on Romans* (London, SCM, 1980), p. 236.

unredeemed humanity and that for which it speaks and whose agony it shares. In other words, the Church is the place, or should be the place, where both the rule of Christ over the world and the inseparable oneness of Christ with the world, expressed by the head–body image, are coming into realization.

Christ is the 'beginning' or, as the NEB puts it more interpretatively, the Church's 'origin', by being 'the first-born from the dead' (verse 18*bc*; cf. Acts 26.23, and esp. Rev. 1.5). This term *archē* is also one which has just been used in the plural of heavenly powers (which perhaps suggests that one of the uses of the term was not an original part of the hymn), and in the related Rev. 3.14 it is appropriately translated 'the prime source (of all God's creation)' (also NEB). The decision to supply 'its' before 'origin' in Col. 1.18*b* is correct if one is to make sense of the flow of the passage as it stands, however much the term *archē* may stem ultimately from a context in which it referred to the 'beginning' or 'origin' of all creation (cf. Prov. 8.22 referred to above and Gen. 1.1). It is of the 'beginning', in the sense of the source and first principle,[14] of a new creation that this part of the hymn now speaks, and that new creation both began with the rising of Jesus as 'the first fruits of those who have fallen asleep' and continues in the newness of life bestowed by him who became in his resurrection 'a life-giving spirit' (1 Cor. 15.20, 45).

Although there are those who regard 'that he might be pre-eminent in everything' or 'amongst all [things?]' (18*d*) as a later addition to the original hymn it seems to supply as good a transition to the statement of 1.19 as 18*bc* does. It is difficult to see why the clause should have been inserted at this point rather than, say, at the end of verse 20. It is at the same time the more succinct equivalent within the Colossians hymn of the affirmation of Christ's exaltation in the Philippians hymn in Phil. 2.9–11.

[14]  The fragmentary text of the Derveni papyrus (13.14 – see ch. 1, n. 37) seems to link 'head' in the Orphic hymn with *archē*; cf. also 15.10 and Kern, *Orph. fr.*, 21*a* and 168.6: Zeus as 'leader (*archos*) of all'. It is also worth comparing Philo, *Vit. Mos.*, 2.60, where Noah is described as the *archē* of a second *genesis* of human beings.

However, it was not just as any individual person whom God happened to raise from the dead that Christ has achieved this pre-eminence, but rather he has achieved it because of what he was and what God has done through him (Col. 1.19–20). For 'in him all the fullness (*plērōma*) was pleased to dwell' (1.19). In 2.9 the phrase 'all the fullness' recurs, but this time qualified by the genitive 'of divine nature', and this is presumably how the writer understands it in 1.19 too; certainly many translations supply 'of God' here. Yet the fact that it is not added here to explain this otherwise enigmatic expression is still surprising, and this in itself may help to support the suggestion that the writer of Colossians is here quoting a source (but probably not a phrase used by his opponents). But what does 'all the fullness' mean? It is argued that it has primarily an active sense rather than a passive one, that which fills rather than that which is filled; 2.10 helps to confirm that, for there, because that which fills dwelt in Christ, those who are in him are in their turn filled (also presumably with deity). However Pokorný argues against limiting the choice to these two alternatives, active and passive: the term rather means the 'fullness of God's will and activity, the perfection that radiates out'.[15] Yet in this sense the term is still very much active, even dynamic, rather than passive. In the Old Testament God is one who fills heaven and earth (Jer. 23.24; cf. Isa. 6.3; Ps. 103.24 LXX), that is, is present in them; and in the New Testament we receive from Christ's fullness (John 1.16), which as in Col. 2.9–10 suggests that, because Christ has received 'fullness', he is able to 'fill' those who receive it from him. It is probably preferable to set this use of the term against such a Judaeo-Christian background, rather than against a (Valentinian) Gnostic one, where, as Lohse notes,[16] the supreme God is usually distinct from the *plērōma*, which is 'the uppermost pneumatic world in immediate proximity to God'. The use of this term in Colossians and Ephesians

---

[15] *Der Brief des Paulus an die Kolosser*, THKNT 10/1 (Berlin, Evangelische Verlagsanstalt, 1987), *p.* 55.

[16] Ibid. p. 57. Pokorný further notes that a Gnostic interpretation of the first strophe of the hymn would be difficult, for there the relation between Creator and Redeemer is a positive one (p. 55).

may well, however, have been the starting-point for later (Christian) Gnostic speculation.

The translation given above in fig. 1 takes 'all the fullness' as the subject of the verb 'was pleased'. However some would supply God as the subject of this verb, although there is little to prepare us for such an insertion, and they would make 'all the fullness' the subject of 'dwell'. Yet the verb 'was pleased', *eudokein*, when followed by an infinitive as here, usually has one subject for both itself and the following infinitive,[17] and in the New Testament it is always the one who is pleased who is also the one who also does what he or she is pleased to do. However, such decisions are made by persons, and a decision like the present one could only be made by God. In that case 'all the fullness' must be a circumlocution for God, in the fullness of the divine grace and power.

When was that decision made and executed? The context surely suggests that, if anything, the moment of Christ's resurrection is meant, although it is not expressly stated.[18] Certainly the tense here is a past one, although 2.9 uses the present tense, 'dwells'. This need not be a contradiction, for the past decision to take up residence is the presupposition for a present occupation. Here, too, we must beware of later dogmatic formulations which could lead us to say that *plērōma* cannot refer to the fullness of the divine nature, for that was in Christ from eternity and thus could not be said to have taken up abode in Christ at any point of time; that argument assumes that the writer of this passage shared later Christians' rejection of adoptionist ideas and thus could not have said that God 'adopted' an already existing being in order to dwell in it. What is perhaps more significant is the way in which the language of these two verses might equally well support what some call an 'inspiration Christology' rather than an incar-

---

[17] So in the oft-quoted parallel to this passage, Ps. 67.17 LXX (= 68.16), 'God was pleased to dwell on it (the holy mountain).' (But note 2 Macc. 14.35; Polybius 1.8.4.) Arguably this understanding of the syntax presents fewer problems when one comes to the second dependent infin., 'to reconcile'; for does it make much sense to say that God was pleased that the whole fullness should reconcile everything?

[18] With this compare Rom. 1.4, esp. if 'in power' is a later addition to the tradition that originally lay behind 1.3–4.

national one.[19] As soon as one interprets the term 'fullness' here
as referring to 'the whole fullness of the power of grace ...
which makes life out of death possible'[20] or 'the authority and
power of God which is at work through the bearer in whom it is
concentrated',[21] then one can see how 'inspiration' well describes the manifestation of this power both in the gracious life
of Jesus on earth and in the life which he now lives in the power
of the spirit of the God who raised him from the dead (cf. Rom.
8.11), a life which manifests God's new creation both in his life
and in the lives of those who walk in newness of life (cf. Rom.
6.4), who share the 'fullness' in him. In fact Pokorný goes a
stage further and, using the ties between Colossians and Mark's
description of Jesus' baptism, argues that 'the *plērōma* is here in
some respects treated as the Holy Spirit. So God's Spirit in all
its fullness has taken Jesus for its dwelling.'[22] But, if so, the
context seems to suggest that Jesus' resurrection, not his
baptism, is the moment of this choice (cf. Rom. 1.4).

Even if Col. 1.18b–20 describes Christ's role in God's new
creation as opposed to his role in the original creation outlined in verses 15–18a, it is still clear that the former is as all-
embracing as the latter: 'all things' are reconciled, and not just
a small portion of humanity or even the whole of humanity.[23]
This reconciliation takes place 'through' Christ and 'for' Christ
(1.20). Christ functions both as the means of reconciliation and
as the goal or purpose of the reconciliation, if the prepositional
phrases in this verse have the same sense as they do in 1.16. (It
is conceivable that this verse is so awkward to translate because
a statement about the new creation in the risen Christ has been

---

[19] E.g. J. P. Mackey in J. D. G. Dunn and J. P. Mackey, *New Testament in Dialogue*
(London, SPCK, 1987), p. 88. Indeed the hymn seems to 'ignore the incarnation
almost entirely' (Pokorný, *Kol.* (n. 15), p. 59).

[20] Schweizer, *Col.* (ch. 1 n. 5), p. 78.

[21] Pokorný, *Kol.* (n. 15), p. 54.

[22] Ibid. p. 71.

[23] The thought of the verse is somewhat confused by the 'through him' and 'to' or 'for
him', which most English translations take to refer respectively to Christ and to God
– even in the ET of Schweizer's *Col.* – despite the fact that both phrases also occur in
1.16f referring to Christ – cf. Houlden, *Letters* (ch. 1 n. 32), p. 173. For this reason I
have kept the 'for him' of 1.16 in verse 20; note that 'reconcile to' is usually
*katallassein* with the dat., not with *eis* and the accus.

modelled upon the statement in verse 16 about the creation that took place in the pre-existent Christ, a statement and formulation that in turn had its ultimate origins within the very different thought-world of Stoicism and could only with difficulty be transferred to the personal deity of the Judaeo-Christian tradition, and with even greater difficulty to the historical figure of Jesus.) What had been intended for creation is now, after a fall (which is, however, never mentioned within this passage), realized in a new creation that takes place in and through Christ and finds its purpose and consummation in him.[24]

If 'all the fullness' (neuter) is the subject of 'was pleased', then the following masculine participle, 'having made peace', confirms that the author understood this 'fullness' as a circumlocution for God and has made the participle agree with its sense rather than its grammatical gender. Just as Paul saw reconciliation as having been achieved through Christ's death (Rom. 5.10), so too God, who is also for Paul the one who reconciles (2 Cor. 5.19),[25] has achieved peace through Christ's blood shed on the cross (Col. 1.20).

### THE THEOLOGY OF COLOSSIANS AND THE HYMN

If it is true that 'Col[ossians] develops its Christology on the basis of the Christ-hymn',[26] it is also true that the author is not

---

[24] It might be tempting to see 'all the fullness' as synonymous with 'all things' at least in an earlier version of the strophe, but 2.9 indicates that the author of Col. understood it as referring to the Creator or an aspect of the Creator rather than to the creation. And to speak of creation 'delighting' to dwell in Christ would be a novel idea; as long as this verb is retained, then God, or a reference to God, must be the subject.

[25] If the active *apokatēllaxen* is read in 1.22 then possibly Christ is the subject, although that is not certain since the second *auton* in the verse must refer to God (and without the active form of the verb it is very difficult to understand the construction of the following infin., 'to present', although J. B. Lightfoot, *Saint Paul's Epistles to the Colossians and to Philemon* (London, Macmillan, 1884[7]), p. 161, daringly suggests that it is dependent still on the *eudokēsen* of 1.19, and treats the passive *apokatallagēte*, a variant reading in 1.22 which is hard to explain as a secondary corruption (cf. *TCGNT*, pp. 621–2), as an alternative to the participial construction of 1.21, as in 1.26 – or perhaps we should regard it as parenthetical).

[26] Lohse, *Col.* (n. 10), p. 178; P. Müller, *Die Anfänge der Paulusschule, dargestellt am zweiten Thessalonicherbrief und am Kolosserbrief*, ATANT 74 (Zürich, Theologischer, 1988), p. 133, goes further: 'The hymn in 1.15–20 colours the whole letter' (cf. also pp. 276–7 – some of his detected allusions to the hymn may be somewhat tenuous).

limited to, or bound by, that which is in the hymn, even in the hymn once it has been through its various stages of modification. Rather he or she selects various elements from it, both Christological and others, which are then developed according to the author's own taste and judgment. The exposition of the hymn to be found within the following chapters is in fact a reinterpretation of it, with different nuances and emphases. Indeed a further argument for the author's having quoted a hymn in 1.15–20 lies in the fact that at a number of points that author's own ideas and interests differ from those contained in the passage, or at least place the emphases somewhat differently, even if it may be going too far to call them corrections of it. It is also helpful to look more carefully at these points of divergence, since they help to bring the author's own concerns and perspectives into sharper focus.

## The 'Body of Christ'

We have already seen that in Col. 2.9 the author of Colossians picks up again the Christological assertions of the hymn: the Colossians are not to be lured away by 'philosophy and empty deceit according to human tradition and according to the elements of the world rather than according to Christ' (2.8). That would be a mistake, for 'all the fullness of divine nature dwells in him *sōmatikōs*, and you are being "filled" in him who is head over every principality and authority' (2.9–10). The argument is a cogent one, particularly if the 'principalities and authorities' (1.16) are connected with the 'elements': the Colossians should not be led astray by following the latter, for they should rather be guided by Christ who is head over them, a domination which by implication they share if they are 'filled' in him. It would add further point to the argument if being 'filled' were a preoccupation of the 'philosophy and vain deceit'. It may be significant that the writer has already expressed a desire that they should be 'filled' with a knowledge of God's will (1.9), but perhaps even more that they are warned against those who are ' "puffed up" without reason by [their] fleshly mind' (2.18). Paul too speaks of the Corinthians who prided themselves on their spiritual endowments, particularly their knowledge, as being 'puffed up' (1 Cor. 4.6, 18–19; 5.2; 8.1), and it is therefore tempting to see the use of this term in Colossians as a similar jibe at a claim to spiritual gifts that included the visions mentioned in 2.18.[27] 2.10 would then be asserting that Christians' true fullness comes from Christ, and in him they are truly 'filled' and have no need of the experiences which others claimed were necessary, either to supplement him or as a superior rival to him.

We have also seen that 2.9 picks up the term 'fullness' from 1.19 and qualifies it by 'of divine nature'. That is a clear indication of how the author of Colossians understands the term in 1.19; it does not rule out the possibility that it had a sense nearer to that of 'all things' at some earlier stage in the development of the thought of this passage, but we cannot recover that stage with any certainty, nor is it how the author understands it in its present form. Moreover, as J.-N. Aletti notes, one would have to explain why a different term was used for the 'all things' found elsewhere in the passage, particularly since the noun *plērōma* is not a technical term in Stoic philosophy or any earlier potential background of thought, however much the cognate verb *plēroō*, 'fill', may have been used.[28]

The other addition that 2.9 makes to 1.19 is the adverb *sōmatikōs* which has been variously translated as 'as an organized body', 'expressing itself through the Body', 'actually', 'in essence', or 'assuming a bodily form'.[29] It has been suggested that this is a counter to a docetic denial of the reality of the incarnation,[30] but there is little firm evidence that such a

---

[27] There is perhaps another ironic jibe at the Colossians' claims to fullness in 2.23 in the word *plēsmonē* there; cf. Bornkamm's paraphrase: 'While that has the appearance of wisdom (namely, following the *dogmata*) – one calls that "voluntary service", "humility", "curbing the body" – yet it has nothing whatever to do with "honor" and serves (only) to glut the flesh' (in Meeks–Francis, *Conflict* (ch. 1 n. 25), p. 143 n. 37).

[28] *Colossiens 1:15–20* (ch. 1 n. 30), p. 80.

[29] Reff. in C. F. D. Moule, *The Epistles to the Colossians and to Philemon*, CGTC (Cambridge University Press, 1958), pp. 92–3.

[30] 'Docetic', from the Greek *dokeō*, I seem, relates to the view that Christ only *seemed* to be human.

view was a problem in Colossae. *If* there is a polemical reference in the addition of this adverb, then it is more likely to be as
a counter to the ascetic tendencies which the letter criticizes.
The writer would then be insisting that Christ possesses the
fullness of divine nature in a bodily form as an implicit criticism of a view that the body must be suppressed, even left
behind, for enjoyment of the powers and the life of the world
above. In contrast, however, to 1.19 Col. 2.9 uses the present
tense, 'dwells'. If that change is significant it would presumably refer to the existence of the risen Christ as still a
corporeal one (cf. 1 Cor. 15.44), although not in the 'body of
flesh' of 1.22. After all, we saw that it was likely that it was in
the resurrected Christ that the 'fullness' had been pleased to
dwell in 1.19.

The suggestion that *sōmatikōs* might be a reference to the
collective 'body of Christ', the Church, would have been more
plausible had not 2.10, after seemingly signalling that it was
using just such an image by introducing the idea of Christ as
the head (cf. 1.18*a*), gone on to speak of Christ as head, not of a
body, the Church, but over principalities and authorities, even
though the text has just spoken of Christ's 'filling' Christians.
Although the author seems able, as we have seen, to slide from
the one sense to the other, we should still distinguish them, for,
as Gnilka puts it,[31] 'according to the one [Christ] is as head the
nourisher and life-giver of the body, the other refers to his
position of dominance'. 'Head' thus seems to be an image that
the author can use in more than one sense; the same is surely
true of 'body' as well in 2.17.[32] For the development of the

---

[31] *Kol.* (ch. 1 n. 8), p. 131.
[32] Unless we can, somehow, see a corporate reference there; the contrast with 'shadow'
(cf. Philo, *Conf. ling.*, 190; *Migr.*, 12) suggests that this would be forced, just as it is
difficult to see *sōmatikōs* being used in 2.9 in a sense analogous to 2.17 without any
corresponding 'shadow'. Schweizer's suggestion (*Col.* (ch. 1 n. 5), p. 157) that a
nom. originally stood in place of the gen. 'of Christ' in 2.17 is daring, but it at least
points towards the likely sense and away from a reference to the collective 'body of
Christ'. However P. Benoit sees here a word-play: it does not say 'the body is Christ',
and so another sense, that of the risen body of Christ, is introduced; 'the body is the
body of Christ' ('Corps, tête et plérome dans les épîtres de la captivité', in Benoit,
*Exégèse et théologie* (Paris, Cerf, 1961), pp. 107–53, here p. 115 n. 1); it must be
granted that a *to* could easily have dropped out before *tou*: 'the body (reality) is that
of Christ'.

imagery of the Church as the body dependent upon the head
we have to wait until 2.19. There the author, using the physio-
logy of the day, speaks of 'the whole body, with all its joints and
ligaments', receiving its supplies from the head, and so, 'linked
together', growing as God intended it. They will then enjoy the
peace, to which they were called, 'in one body' (3.15). This
'body' is not, therefore, an entity already complete in itself, but
one that grows and is still being 'filled' (2.10).

However, the idea that the 'body' was the Church (1.18a)
was also referred to earlier in Colossians, in 1.24, in one of the
more enigmatic verses of the entire New Testament:[33] the
writer suffers on the Colossians' behalf and 'fills up' or 'com-
pletes (antanapleroō) what is lacking' or 'what remains of
Christ's sufferings ... for the sake of his body, which is the
Church'. By opting for 'what remains' rather than 'what is
lacking' as a translation of hysterēmata one at least mitigates one
problem, the possible implication that somehow Christ's sufferings had been deficient or insufficient. One then needs to ask,
as Schweizer notes,[34] what is the force of the first prepositional
prefix of the verb, anti-: on whose behalf or in whose place is the
'filling up' or 'completing' done? On behalf of Christ or on
behalf of, in place of, the Church? Schweizer favours the latter,
and makes the further point that the word translated 'sufferings' here (thlipseis) is never used of Christ's passion (whereas
that used of the apostle's afflictions in this verse, pathēmata, can
be: Phil. 3.10). He also draws attention to 2 Cor. 1.4–5, where,
in the words of K. T. Kleinknecht, 'Paul describes his affliction
(thlipsis) as an abounding (perisseuein) of the sufferings of Christ
to us (pathēmata tou Christou eis hēmas)'.[35] Kleinknecht sees in the
Pauline writings the idea that Christ's sufferings and those of
Paul and the Church are alike the result of the hostility to
which God's righteous one(s) would be exposed in the

---

[33] It has even attracted a monograph devoted to the history of its interpretation:
J. Kremer, Was an den Leiden Christi noch mangelt: eine interpretationsgeschichtliche und
exegetische Untersuchung zu Kol. 1,24b, BBB 12 (Bonn, Hanstein, 1956).
[34] Col. (ch. 1 n. 5), p. 103.
[35] Der leidende Gerechtfertigte: die alttestamentlich-jüdische Tradition vom 'leidenden Gerechten'
und ihre Rezeption bei Paulus, WUNT 2.13 (Tübingen, Mohr, 1984), pp. 377–8; cf.
p. 245.

end-time. However, the argument of Lightfoot is still persuasive that the words here are more naturally understood of a
completing of sufferings on Christ's behalf, in Christ's place, for
the *hysterēmata* are in Christ's sufferings, not the Church's.[36] Yet
that need not refer to Christ's passion, but to the sufferings
which now afflict those who now stand for him in this hostile
world, his body, the Church, and above all the apostle who
speaks in his name and as a consequence suffers in his name.
The easiest solution to the problems of the present verse thus
seems to lie along the lines of seeing Colossians as here taking a
step beyond Paul's ideas: it regards the afflictions (*thlipseis*)
suffered by the Church, and above all by the apostle on its
behalf (cf. also 2 Cor. 4.12), as Christ's sufferings too, for the
Church is Christ's body as the verse goes on to say. So Christ
must go on suffering as his people suffer, and so sufferings
remain for him and were not finished with his crucifixion. But
the apostle endures his sufferings for the Church's sake, for, as
1.25 asserts, the apostle's divinely ordained role is to serve the
Church, and that service involves suffering in order to bring
into being and build up the Church (1.29, *kopiō agōnizomenos*;
cf. 2 Cor. 11.28; Gal. 4.19), in addition to the suffering which is
the lot of all who serve Christ; the apostle's sufferings are 'the
sufferings which are of necessity involved in building up God's
kingdom (the preaching of God's word), since Satan would like
to destroy Christ's work'.[37] Knowing of the apostle's struggle
(*agōn*) on their behalf the Colossians and Laodiceans and
others will be encouraged (2.1–2).

### Reconciliation – cosmic or personal?

We have seen that the hymn persistently refers to the creation
and reconciliation of 'all things' (neuter) through Christ (1.16,
17, ?18, 20). 'The cosmic Christology in the first strophe is
matched by a cosmic soteriology in the second.'[38] But just as

---

[36] *Col.* (n. 25), pp. 164–5.
[37] Kremer, *Leiden Christi*, p. 174.
[38] H. Hegermann, *Die Vorstellung vom Schöpfungsmittler im hellenistischen Judentum und
Urchristentum*, TU 82 (Berlin, Akademie, 1961), p. 101.

persistently the author of Colossians, both before (1.13–14) and after the hymn, speaks of the redemption and reconciliation of *people*. The 'and you' of 1.21 may indeed be dependent on the verb 'reconcile' in verse 20, if we treat the former as part of the same sentence as 1.9–20, as J. B. Lightfoot does,[39] in contrast to most modern translators and commentators, who find the flowing sentence of verses 9–20 long enough as it is! If the cosmic dimensions of the hymn are retained at all in 1.21–3 it is in the fact that the gospel telling of this reconciliation is proclaimed 'in all of creation that is under heaven'. But now it is heard by people, and 'all creation' is limited to the realm 'under heaven' and no longer includes the heavenly realm as was the case in 1.20 and even more emphatically in 1.16.

Thus, while the hymn is in essence truly universal in scope, the concerns of the author of the letter narrow this scope down and focus upon the reconciliation of human beings accomplished in Christ. Christ is still God's 'mystery', God's secret now revealed (cf. 2.2), but it is Christ among the nations of the world (1.27), not the Christ in whom are all things (neuter). That concern continues through into chapter 2, which speaks of people's transgressions being forgiven (2.13), and of the bond against them being obliterated (2.14). The presupposition of the moral exhortations of 3.5ff. is not the new creation of all things, but the creation of a new human being that is being renewed in knowledge according to the image (*kat' eikona*) of its Creator (3.10). It could be that the whole phrase 'in the image of' simply expresses a relationship and is equivalent to 'like'. Yet Christ has been described in 1.15 as that 'image', and so it is perhaps preferable to find the relationship solely in the preposition *kata*, and to see here a deliberate reference back to Christ as the 'image', as proclaimed in the hymn. This may be the reason for the difference here to the otherwise very similar passage, Gal 3.27–8, where Christians put on Christ. Here they put on a new humanity made according to God's image, and that image is Christ. It is that humanity which is being renewed (present tense) in knowledge. That

---

[39] *Col.* (n. 25), p. 160. Many edd. even begin a new paragraph at 1.21, but Westcott and Hort's edition only has a colon after 1.20.

new human who was Christ could not so naturally be said to be still being renewed in knowledge. Confirmation of this echo of the hymn may also be found in the following verse:[40] in that new creation divisions of humanity are transcended and superseded, and Christ is 'all things and in all [things?]'. Here the author reverts to the neuter plurals of the hymn, despite the anthropocentricity of this passage.

Finally, we also read in 3.15 that 'peace' is to rule in the Colossians' hearts, and that to this they were called in one body. Apart from the further reference to the one (collective) body, the Church, this is also the only other reference to 'peace' in the letter apart from the use of the compound verb, 'make peace', in 1.20, and Schillebeeckx therefore argues that 'cosmic peace [referred to in 1.20] has *now* in fact *already* been realized, but for the moment only in the community of the Church, Christ's sphere of power'.[41] If peace rules, arbitrates (*brabeuein*; a compound of this verb is used in 2.18) within the community, it will crown those qualities of heart listed in 3.12–14 which are all ones that promote a healthy community within the Church (in contrast to the list of vices in verses 8–9 which are ones that would poison their interpersonal relations). The community of the Church is to be, as it were, a microcosm of the cosmic peace and reconciliation apparently proclaimed in the hymn (1.20).

It is in keeping with this that it is widely agreed that the author of Colossians has taken the cosmic concept of the body found in the hymn and has interpreted it consistently of the Church, and has similarly taken the cosmic redemption of the hymn and has narrowed its scope down to the redemption of people. That presents us with a hermeneutical problem: is the scope narrowed in this way because the writer disapproves of the cosmic dimension, or simply because he or she is not interested in it or does not grasp the full implications of it? If the hymn were a passage used by those being countered in the

---

40 Loosely attached to the preceding by *hopou*, a figurative 'where' meaning 'a new creation of humanity in which ... '

41 *Christ* (ch. 1 n. 41), p. 191; italics his; cf. also p. 194 – this is not just 'peace for the soul'.

letter then it might be plausible to see the author of the letter
here hoisting them with their own petard. One could then
argue that he or she sees the hymn as true only as it is
reinterpreted in Colossians. Yet it is hard to see how this
hymn, however its original form is reconstructed, would be
consonant with the sort of preoccupation with angelic powers
that is a likely characteristic of the opponents. It is therefore
likelier that the writer uses it as an expression of the faith
which he or she shares with the readers of the letter. It is
therefore open to us to say that there are further depths of
meaning in the passage which the writer has not plumbed, but
which we may plumb with some confidence that we are not
thereby using this text perversely or in a way that runs
directly counter to the author's intention in quoting it. But
whether we will be altogether happy with what we bring up
from those deeper depths is quite another matter, as we shall
see (chapter 4).

### Crucifixion and resurrection

One reason for treating 1.20*b* as a later addition to an original
strophe which spoke of Christ achieving reconciliation in a new
creation accomplished in his resurrection from the dead is the
way in which the thoroughly Pauline stress on the cross is
suddenly introduced. For from verse 18*b* onwards the focus is
neither on his incarnation nor on his death, but on his role as
first-born from the dead. In 20*b* the crucifixion, as the moment
and means of reconciliation, is introduced for the first time, in
keeping with Paul's thought, as we saw in the previous section,
and it is this that is developed in the exposition and application
of the hymn which follows immediately afterwards in 1.21–3:
there reconciliation is again achieved through Christ's death
(verse 22), and it is again in his death that he wins his victory
according to 2.14–15.

These latter verses speak of what God has accomplished
through Christ's cross in striking terms unparalleled in the
New Testament, and at times puzzling in their imagery. On
the cross God (who is apparently still the subject of the sen-

tence, carrying on from verse 13) has wiped out a bond, a handwritten (legal) document (like a holograph in modern legal parlance). Something of the background to this image can be seen in Philemon 19, where Paul speaks of his writing down his obligation, his debt to Philemon, with his own hand. He will repay it. But there one knows who is writing the document. Who has written the one which God has now annulled? Many tend to identify this 'bond' with the Jewish Law or with a set of legal demands of some sort, and therefore to translate the following dative, *tois dogmasin*, as, perhaps, a dative of accompanying circumstances: 'with its legal demands'. In that case the implication is that God or the angelic powers have written this document and have set it against the account of humanity. However, the parallel in Philemon 19 and other uses of this term suggest that its normal sense is that one writes such a document against oneself, as it were, committing oneself legally to repay a debt or to do something else of that kind; the document is regarded more as a 'promissory note'[42] which looks forward to future repayment rather than as a statement of an indebtedness incurred in the past, although the one may often, but not always (Philemon 19), entail the other. Dealing with past failures is clearly meant by the forgiveness of transgressions in verse 13. The NEB offers here a translation that accords with this line of interpretation better than most: 'he has cancelled the bond which pledged us to the decrees of the law',[43] or they are the recipients of the promise implicit in the idea of the *cheirographon* as a 'promissory note'. Colossians then states that by God's action through Christ we are released from our obligation to keep that promise, rather than from, say, our fear and anxiety at not having kept it or at the threat of punishment levelled by some heavenly record of our misdeeds that another

---

[42] E. Lohse in *TDNT*, vol. 9, p. 435 (so the ET, but his subsequent interpretation of the image follows the very different connotations of the original *Schuldschein*).

[43] Behind this translation perhaps lies an interpretation like that of J. A. T. Robinson (*The Body: a Study in Pauline Theology*, SBT 5 (London, SCM, 1952), p. 43 n. 1) and others that the dative *tois dogmasin* is an indirect object of the verb 'to write' implicit in the term for 'bond' used here, *cheirographon*. In, e.g., *P. Tebt.*, 48.5 the cognate verb *cheirographein* is followed by a dat.

has compiled.[44] In other words, even if the obliterating of past
transgressions was a theme in verse 13, verse 14 concentrates to
a greater degree on the positive aspect of the new life mentioned in that verse, a new life that involves freedom from
obligation to keep legal requirements (cf. Rom. 7.1–6). Something of the same blend of retrospect and prospect, negative
and positive, occurs in Rom. 4.25: Christ has dealt with our
transgressions *and* offers us that new life which is justification.

God did this by removing the bond and nailing it to the cross
(2.14). It is dangerous to press the imagery here. Christ himself
was certainly nailed to a cross and so too, if we can believe the
Gospel accounts, was possibly a brief but mocking indication of
the charge on which he was crucified, that of being king of the
Jews (Mark 15.26 and parallels). The interpretation just
offered of the nature of the 'bond' is not particularly close to
either of these, for it is neither the debtor nor the charge against
the debtor as such, except in so far as an acknowledged debt, if
unpaid, is a charge against one. But if it is an obligation to keep
certain requirements that is here removed then this is close in
sense to what Paul means by 'dying to the Law' (Gal. 2.19; cf.
Rom. 7.4, 6), even if Colossians never uses that somewhat
ambiguous construction with the dative.[45]

If the imagery is already mixed in 2.14 the metaphor certainly changes again in 2.15, but the question is how consistent
the imagery is within that verse. It clearly ends with a reference
to the Roman triumph in which the victorious leader paraded
captives and spoils of war before the populace of Rome. It is
therefore tempting to see this image operating throughout the
verse, and thus to translate the participle *apekdysamenos* at the
start of it as active in sense, 'disarm', 'deprive of power'. This
would fit in well with the following *edeigmatisen*, 'exposed to
mockery', although W. Carr takes this in a neutral sense and
sees Christ as parading the powers as a Roman general would

---

[44] Although this sense is attested for *cheirographon* in *Apoc. Zephaniah*, 3.6–9; cf. *OTP*, vol.
1, p. 511; *The Apocryphal Old Testament*, ed. H. F. D. Sparks (Oxford, Clarendon
Press, 1984), p. 921.

[45] Contrast Col. 2.20 – dying *apo* + the gen.; cf. also Wedderburn, *Baptism* (ch. 1 n. 3),
p. 43 n. 1.

lead his own troops.[46] However, the same verb does occur in 3.9 in a middle or reflexive sense, used of stripping off the old humanity from oneself like a discarded suit, and the cognate noun, *apekdysis*, seems to be used in a similar way immediately before in 2.11 of the stripping off (oneself) of the body of flesh. Moreover, this particular compound, both verb and noun, does not seem to occur in Greek literature before Colossians; how likely is it that the author would introduce a pair of seeming new coinages, but in two different senses? If we retain the reflexive sense here then the image would apparently be that of Christ laying off the powers which he wore as part of the garment of the old nature. That in turn would be the more plausible if the 'circumcision of Christ' of 2.11, the 'stripping off of the body of flesh', were not only a reference to what Christians do in baptism, but also implied that Christ himself, and with him those whom he represents, had 'stripped off the body of flesh' and had thus been 'circumcised' in his death on the cross with 'the most radical form' of circumcision.[47] However, this line of interpretation of 2.15 becomes impossible if indeed God is still the subject of the sentence in verse 15, for it is hard to conceive of any way in which God could be thought to wear the heavenly powers and strip them off in Christ's crucifixion.[48] Moreover it must be granted that giving an active sense to *apekdysamenos* ('disarm', 'deprive of power') makes the imagery of the verse far clearer, and as long as there is the possibility that the author is again quoting, or even just echoing, traditional material here, as many suggest, it is quite possible that the source used this word in a somewhat different sense to that of the author of Colossians.

The introduction of a mention of the cross into the context of cosmic 'reconciliation' or the defeat of heavenly powers creates

---

46 *Angels and Principalities*, SNTSMS 42 (Cambridge University Press, 1981), pp. 63–5; this involves a difficult change of subject and an unusual sense of *edeigmatisen*.

47 J. Lähnemann, *Der Kolosserbrief: Komposition, Situation und Argumentation*, SUNT 3 (Gütersloh, Mohn, 1971), pp. 121–2.

48 To treat verse 15 as referring still to God's actions helps with the difficulty of deciding whether the last two words of the verse mean 'in him' (Christ) or 'on it' (the cross). If Christ is the subject of the verse, one is perhaps forced to choose the latter, however awkward, but if God is the subject 'in Christ' is not only more natural but perfectly possible.

considerable difficulties. For, if theologians have wrestled long
with the problem of explaining adequately how the death of
Jesus 'saved' humanity, yet at least the saving significance of
that death for humanity seems to have made some sense
within the categories of first-century thought. Animals and
martyrs were thought to die in order to benefit people by
atoning for sins. However, L. Hartman has pointed out how
the idea of bringing harmony to one's whole world also lay
close at hand in many cultic ideas and symbols of the time.
One's offerings to the gods brought peace with those who
controlled one's natural environment.[49] The idea of 'reconciliation' through a resurrection is a different one again, and is
even harder to parallel, but one can see how such an event,
viewed as a new creation, essentially an event of similarly
cosmic proportions as the initial creation, or as the first-fruits
of a new creation, could lead to the idea that this event at least
initiated, and set the pattern for, a reconciliation that would
involve all creation (cf. Rom. 8.11, 19–23; 1 Cor. 15.20–8).
Was this the idea originally found in this passage, and was it
then modified by the insertion of the characteristically Pauline
idea of atonement by Christ's death (in Paul's thought
atonement for people, not the whole of creation)? Both ideas,
reconciliation by Christ's resurrection and reconciliation by
Christ's death, surely involve, however, a considerable shift in
thought from the concept of a mediation of peace by wisdom,
i.e. a quality of the creator God, a mediation that has preserved the world from its beginning, to the idea that the death
or resurrection of an individual within history has brought
about such a mediation.

### The 'Powers' – reconciled or vanquished?

Col. 1.20 speaks of the reconciliation of 'all things', be they
things on earth or things in heaven. This description of the 'all
things' clearly echoes 1.16, which, as we saw, was further

---

[49] 'Reconciliation' (ch. 1 n. 16), p. 113; yet, as he notes (p. 114), reconciliation in 1.20
is 'to' Christ, not God. More seriously, the passages which speak of Philo's *logos*
bringing peace to the world do not speak of the *logos* dying to do so.

expanded not only by the pair 'visible and invisible', but also
by the four terms which, it was argued, are different words for
heavenly and invisible powers, even if they have their this-
worldly manifestations.

One would therefore expect that the 'all things' that are
reconciled in verse 20 would also include these powers.
However 1.13 seems to speak of a 'realm of darkness' which still
exists, from which we have been rescued. Is this 'realm' now
reconciled? Has it become 'light'? Moreover the verses immediately following the hymn go on to speak only of the reconciliation of sinful human beings, and 2.15 uses a very different
language and imagery of Christ's relationship to, and
treatment of, these powers: they are exposed to ridicule on the
cross and led as captives in Christ's triumphal procession. The
thought of 1.15–20 would suggest that the powers are at all
times subordinate to Christ, and that his death and resurrection
restores them to a relationship with himself that has been
disturbed by an unmentioned fall or dislocation of the original
harmony. 2.15 is far less eirenic and harmonious in its language
and imagery: its reconciliation, if it can be called that at all, is
rather that of the mailed fist and military might, forcibly
suppressing those opposed to it. Its language is that of violent
confrontation.

Now some try to lessen the tension between these ideas: they
seek, for instance, to interpret the 'reconciliation' of 1.20 in the
light of 2.15, so that 'reconciliation' of the powers 'means more
of what is understood as pacification, an imposing of peace,
something brought about by conquest'.[50] It is true that, if
M. Wolter is right to see behind the terms 'reconcile' and 'make
peace' the ruler-ideology of the time, then pacification may be
a more appropriate term for what is meant here. Yet at the
same time he grants that peace and reconciliation no longer
have simply a political sense, but a cosmic one. The hymn has
brought together two different ideas, that of cosmic strife in
nature and the idea of the divine ruler who now becomes ruler

---

[50] F. F. Bruce, 'Colossian Problems 4: Christ as Conqueror and Reconciler', in *BSac*,
141 (1984), pp. 291–302, here p. 293; cf. Bruce, *Col.*, p. 76.

of the cosmos.[51] That inevitably means a shift in meaning for both images.

However, the author of Colossians does go on to apply precisely the same unusual compound verb, *apokatallassein*, to the reconciliation of people in 1.22. He or she at least is unlikely to understand this use of the verb in the sense of 'pacify', and this is part of Wolter's evidence for his conclusion that 'both clusters of ideas [in the hymn and in the commentary upon it in 1.21–3] start from totally different assumptions and should not be merged with each other': 'redemption', 'blood' and 'forgiveness of sins' do not effect a cosmic reconciliation.[52]

### BAPTISM AND ESCHATOLOGY

At the end of the first part of chapter 1 we saw how not only the insistence on Christ's supremacy over everything (including most especially all heavenly powers), but also the insistence that those who are Christ's already share with him both in the fullness of the divine power that fills him and, by implication, in his superiority over all may have arisen as a response to the suggestion that heavenly powers barred one's way to the heavenly world; one therefore needed to keep in with them if one was ever to make one's way to that world. But in fact, the author of Colossians insists, God has 'rescued us from the realm of darkness and has transferred us to the kingdom of his beloved Son' (1.13), which is here seemingly our final destination and state, rather than the interim kingdom of Christ envisaged in 1 Cor. 15.24–8.

That rescue and transfer, described in the past tense, occurred, in the opinion of many, in baptism, and consequently this passage, and much of the letter, are interpreted as coming from a baptismal setting. So 1.13–14 and the following hymn are described as a 'baptismal liturgy',[53] and baptism is seen as the

---

[51] *Rechtfertigung und zukünftiges Heil: Untersuchungen zu Röm. 5,1–11*, BZNW 43 (Berlin/New York, de Gruyter, 1978), pp. 57–9; he cites particularly appropriately Plut., *De Alexandri magni fortuna et virtute*, 329C where *diallaktēs tōn holōn* is used of Alexander's conquests and subsequent attempts to unify his empire; cf. also Dio C. 73.15.5.

[52] *Rechtfertigung*, p. 60.

[53] E. Käsemann, 'A Primitive Christian Baptismal Liturgy', in *Essays on New Testament Themes*, SBT 41 (London, SCM, 1964), pp. 149–68.

setting of much of the ethical material which the letter contains. Yet there is but one express reference to baptism in the letter, in 2.12, in a clear echo of Rom. 6; however, it could be added that, since we know that a tradition similar to 3.11 occurs in a plainly baptismal context (Gal. 3.27–8), we can regard this passage in Colossians as further evidence for the baptismal context of much of the material in the letter. One could easily see here a reference, too, to the stripping and clothing themselves again of those being baptized. It would be natural to use such imagery to express the new start, the new life begun in the Christian initiation rite.[54] Yet such language, once introduced by the ritual, could take on a life of its own: so Paul in Rom. 13.12–14 could speak of 'laying aside the deeds of darkness' and 'putting on the weapons of light', 'putting on the Lord Jesus Christ'. Here he addresses those who are already Christians and makes no reference in this context to their already having put off the old nature or having put on the new in the rite of baptism.

Therefore caution is advisable here: to say that the ideas or imagery of a passage are appropriate to the context of baptism does not necessarily mean that they were connected with baptism, let alone that they were peculiarly, far less exclusively, at home in that context. Before baptism there was conversion and before that God's saving work in Christ, and after it there is a life to be lived in Christ. Baptism symbolized the former and ceremonially inaugurated the latter. It would be only natural that the imagery and language used of God's work of salvation, of conversion and of the Christian life should both enrich, and in turn be enriched by, the imagery and language of the Christian initiation rite. It is significant that W. Marxsen could argue that even in the case of a passage like Rom. 6 Paul was reflecting, not on the meaning of baptism itself, but rather on the meaning of having been baptized, and thus on the meaning of Christian existence.[55] What one believes about Christian

---

[54] On the evidence for supposing that stripping was from early on part of the baptismal ritual cf. J. Z. Smith, 'The Garments of Shame', in *HR* 5 (1966), pp. 217–38.

[55] 'Erwägungen zur neutestamentlichen Begründung der Taufe', in *Apophoreta*, BZNW 30, ed. W. Eltester and F. H. Kettler (Berlin, Töpelmann, 1964), pp. 169–77, esp. pp. 171–2.

existence should shape one's beliefs about, and performance of, the rite that marks its beginning just as many of the ideas associated with the rite may be appropriate in the description of Christians' lives. To locate a particular image or motif exclusively in the setting of baptism may blind us to the interrelatedness of this rite and what preceded and followed it.

For here, as in Pauline statements concerning dying with Christ, a fundamental assumption is that of the representative nature of Christ's experiences, an assumption that is not tied particularly to the rite of baptism: if he has been exalted and gone to be with God, then so have all those whom he represents. If he is alive, then so are they, and he can be described as their 'life'. This life is 'hidden' inasmuch as Christ is not now visible to the eye. In themselves they are not alive in the sense of enjoying that fullness of being that Christ now enjoys, but they have this in Christ and only in Christ. They are being 'filled in him' (2.10).[56]

However, it is true that there is the one explicit reference to baptism in 2.12. But there may be a particular reason for that. In the first place the author of Colossians extends the thought of Christians dying with Christ, found in Paul's references to baptism in Rom. 6, and also asserts that they have already risen with him, in order to show the Colossians that they have no reason to fear that the heavenly powers might place any impediments in the way of their progress to the world above. For they are already there in a sense, sharing in Christ's exaltation. It is preferable to see this as a logical development of Paul's thought to meet this specific pastoral need, rather than either of the two alternative explanations that have been suggested: these are either (a) to view it as an attempt to correct Rom. 6, where sharing in Christ's resurrection entails only a walking 'in newness of life' in contrast to a future share in his resurrection (if the futures of 6.5 and 8 are taken as purely temporal, as opposed to logical, futures); or (b) to see it as a reversion to an earlier enthusiastic view of baptism, formulated under the influence of a supposed soteriology of the

---

[56] Cf. further Wedderburn, *Baptism* (ch. 1 n. 3), pp. 342–56.

preceding part of the letter (in itself perhaps a hint that traditional material has been quoted) and lead on to an application of this tradition to their lives. In particular this letter applies it to their attitude towards the false teaching that threatens them, a competing and human tradition (2.8). This in turn is backed up by a further assertion of the salvation that is theirs in Christ, introduced by the 'for' (*hoti*) of 2.9, before the detailed consequences of this are introduced by a 'therefore' in 2.16. Then, finally, 3.1–4 combines the statement that their life is 'hidden with Christ in God' with the appeal to seek the things above, where Christ is, and to orientate their thinking and their living around them. Then in 3.5 the author turns to the more detailed practical instruction which the letter contains. For, having once more affirmed that Christians have died with Christ (3.3; cf. 2.12) and have risen with him (3.1; cf. 2.12–13), the author, stating the paradox of indicative and imperative with a sharpness almost unparalleled in Paul's writings,[64] says that 'therefore' they should 'put to death their limbs that are on earth'. Having 'put on' the new humanity (3.10) they are then urged to 'put on' qualities that befit this new humanity (3.12), just as 2.6 had urged them to 'walk' in that Christ Jesus the Lord of whom they had been taught in the Church's tradition. The regulations demanded by the 'philosophy' and the need to keep them, we have seen, have been removed by Christ, our bondage to them finished on the cross (2.14). In their place is a humanity renewed in the likeness of Christ, ruled by his peace and his 'word' (3.15–16). This means that the affirmation of Christ's redeeming work is followed by a call to live out its consequences, not only positively, but also negatively, in that one is no longer to fulfil 'evil works' (1.21) nor even under any obligation to keep the 'regulations' of the competing 'philosophy' (cf. the 'therefore' of 2.16).

The same correlation between what God has already done on their behalf in Christ and the response which this action should evoke is evinced by the way in which the service called for, in word and deed, is described in 3.17 as a 'giving thanks to

[64] Cf. E. Gräßer, 'Kol. 3,1–4 als Interpretation secundum homines recipientes', in *ZTK*, 64 (1964), pp. 139–68, here p. 148.

enjoys the position of lordship set out above all in 1.15–20.[60]
Their role in the present is not to desert their hope (1.23), but
to seek for the things above (3.1), and to have their minds and
lives oriented around that world above (3.2) rather than being
preoccupied with perishable things, human commands and
teachings, things of the flesh (2.22–3). They should rather
await the time when what is hidden in heaven, Christ, will be
made manifest and they themselves with him (3.4). This is not,
however, a call to an other-worldly detachment or disinterest
in life in this world, for the subsequent instructions in 3.5ff. are
very much concerned with the practical living out of a life
'worthy of the Lord' (1.10) here in this world. Indeed, as we
shall see, these instructions do not perhaps sufficiently allow
the world above to transform the structures of this world.

Many scholars have noted here how the temporal categories
more characteristic of Paul's theology have given way to
spatial ones: a distinction of 'now, in the present age' – 'then,
the age (in a large measure still) to come' has at least partially
been replaced by one of 'here on earth' – 'there in heaven'.
Only partially, however, for 3.4 looks towards a future
manifestation of what is still at present hidden, and 3.6, 24–5
retain what W. Schrage calls 'traditional motifs of judgment
and reward' in the future.[61] However, S. Schulz dismisses these
tenses and motifs as just an 'echo of early Christian expectation
of the *parousia*'.[62] Yet these temporal and spatial categories
should not be too sharply distinguished, for Zeilinger plausibly
locates the talk of the mystery now revealed (1.26; 4.4) in the
context of Jewish apocalyptic writings, where God's hidden
plan, to be revealed later to all, is now discernible by the seer in
heaven, perhaps with the aid of an angelic intermediary.[63]
That in turn only serves to underline how Jewish apocalyptic
writings combined both spatial and temporal categories in
their imagery. The author of Colossians probably thus in large

---

[60] Lähnemann, *Kolosserbrief* (n. 47), p. 31, describes 'the things above' in 3.1 as
summarizing the account of Christ's lordship given in chapters 1–2.
[61] *The Ethics of the New Testament* (Edinburgh, Clark, 1988), p. 245.
[62] *Ethik* (ch. 1 n. 54), p. 559.
[63] *Erstgeborene* (ch. 1 n. 23), pp. 94–115.

God the Father' through Christ. This phrase echoes the words of 1.12, 'giving thanks to the Father', that launched the writer upon the ensuing characterization of God's redemptive work and of what has been achieved in the Son. That divine action calls for a thanksgiving, a thanksgiving that accompanies and motivates the Christian's doing all in the name of Christ. At the same time J. T. Sanders is right to note that too great a stress on what has already been bestowed weakens the urgency and cogency of any ethical appeal:[65] if one is already fully saved, does it matter how one acts? Yet in this tension Colossians shares common ground with Paul, except in so far as Paul indicates that salvation cannot be taken for granted (e.g. 1 Cor. 9.27). That is probably a dimension of Christian experience which the writer of Colossians did not want to emphasize in the face of a teaching which stressed the obstacles in the way of a Christian finally attaining salvation.

When it comes to spelling out the 'doing all in the name of Christ', Colossians, Schrage notes, shares Paul's blend of the general and the specific: it is not just the old humanity that is put off, but the old humanity with all its deeds, examples of which are given in the previous verses (3.8–9; cf. 3.5), and similarly putting on the new humanity involves displaying a number of qualities, including those listed in 3.12–14.[66] Schulz goes further: these two humanities are constituted by their respective actions.[67] In specifying how a Christian should behave the letter is apparently guided neither by sayings of Jesus (however much the character of Jesus as remembered in Christian tradition may have determined the qualities expected in a Christian) nor, at least overtly, by the Old Testament, although L. Hartman, Schulz and others see the influence of the Ten Commandments, and Jewish material which interpreted and applied them, on the ethical instructions of the letter, including the 'domestic code'.[68] As in Rom.

---

[65] *Ethics in the New Testament* (London, SCM, 1975), p. 76.
[66] *Ethics* (n. 61), p. 246.
[67] *Ethik* (ch. 1 n. 54), p. 566.
[68] Cf. Schulz in ch. 1 n. 54; Hartman, 'Code and Context; a Few Reflections on the Parenesis of Col. 3:6–4:1', in *Tradition and Interpretation in the New Testament: Essays in*

15.7, however, the gracious, saving actions of Christ provide guidance and motivation for Christians in their conduct towards one another (Col. 3.13): they should forgive each other or treat each other with grace (*charizomai*). From that it is a short step to appeal for love as the crowning quality of Christians' lives (3.14), the 'bond that brings perfection';[69] the close proximity of this appeal to 3.13 renders questionable Sanders' charge that love has here 'lost any definite character'.[70] Love is rather more likely 'Christ-shaped'. And, as in Romans, so here the ways of Christ are invoked to cement together the Church; and it is with the formation and holding together of the Church that the writer is concerned when the qualities are selected that are to be mentioned, for they are all ones which would serve to unite the Church, just as the vices that are to be 'put off' in 3.8–9 are ones that would tear it apart.

That apart, it is not the content of the ethical instructions of Colossians that is specifically Christian, but rather the basis for it to which the writer appeals. That is particularly clear in the list of responsibilities in the 'domestic code' of 3.18–4.1: such conduct is 'fitting in the Lord', 'pleasing in the Lord', is a service of the Lord, shows fear of the Lord in heaven, and looks to the Lord for its reward. Yet is all this any more than lending a Christian endorsement to the thoroughly patriarchal norms of society of the day? (As Schrage notes,[71] only fathers are mentioned in 3.21, and wives are expected to subject themselves to their husbands.) Is it perhaps significant that 3.11 concentrates on ethnic and religious differences as superseded in Christ and, unlike Gal. 3.28, makes no mention of those between the sexes and between slave and free? At the same time the argument of K. Müller should be noted, that the conventions being adopted in Colossians were not universally accepted, but represent a humane middle way between the

---

*Honor of E. Earle Ellis for His 60th Birthday*, ed. G. F. Hawthorne and O. Betz, (Grand Rapids, Eerdmans/Tübingen, Mohr, 1987), pp. 237–47, esp. pp. 239–42.

[69] Treating this as a 'genitive of direction and purpose' (BDF §166) – so BDR p. 137 n. 1.

[70] *Ethics* (n. 65), p. 68.

[71] *Ethics* (n. 61), p. 253.

other options of a harsh reactionary assertion of patriarchal
rights and emancipatory tendencies current in the first century
BCE.[72] All the same an endorsement of the *status quo* would only
be avoided if bringing these conventions under the authority of
the Lord brought about a radical reappraisal of them, a questioning whether these relationships reflected the character of
the Lord. There is little sign in Colossians of that happening (it
lacks even the mutual subordination found in Eph. 5.21),[73]
except perhaps in the call for husbands to love their wives; yet
even this, Schulz suggests,[74] is merely conventional. When this
questioning does not occur the consequences are calamitous: as
Schweizer shows in a brief survey of the later development of
this tradition,[75] what should be a common subjection of all to
their one Lord turns into a fixed, hierarchical and patriarchal
order, a sanctification of the *status quo*. There is, as Balch puts
it,[76] 'a movement toward what is more common in contemporary Hellenistic household ethics, losing what is most unusual'.

[72] 'Die Haustafel des Kolosserbriefes und das antike Frauenthema: eine kritische
Rückschau auf alte Ergebnisse', in *Theologisches Jahrbuch* (1986), pp. 150–90.

[73] Sanders, *Ethics* (n. 65), p. 75, describes these codes (in Eph. and 1 Pet. as well as
Col.) as 'completely worthless for Christian ethics'.

[74] *Ethik* (ch. 1 n. 54), p. 569; he finds the fact that children are addressed at all as
persons more unusual. F. Laub, 'Sozialgeschichtlicher Hintergrund und ekklesiolo-
gische Relevanz der neutestamentlich-frühchristlichen Haus- und Gemeinde-
Tafelparänese – ein Beitrag zur Soziologie des Frühchristentums', in *MTZ*, 37
(1986), pp. 249–72, finds this true also of the way that slaves are addressed; the
treatment of wives, children and slaves as equally members of the Church shows the
unusual power of the Church to integrate all persons.

[75] *Col.* (ch. 1 n. 5), pp. 217–20; cf. the fuller account in his 'Die Weltlichkeit des Neuen
Testaments: die Haustafeln', in Schweizer, *Neues Testament* (ch. 1 n. 40),
pp. 194–210, esp. pp. 204–10, and 'Traditional Ethical Patterns in the Pauline and
Post-Pauline Letters and Their Development (Lists of Vices and House-Tables)', in
*Text and Interpretation: Studies in the New Testament Presented to Matthew Black*, ed.
E. Best and R. McL. Wilson (Cambridge University Press, 1979), pp. 195–209;
here it is clearer that he sees Colossians as avoiding most of the pitfalls of this ethical
tradition into which later Christian documents fell.

[76] 'Codes' (ch. 1 n. 53), p. 47.

# CHAPTER 3

# Colossians, the Pauline Corpus and the theology of the New Testament

This study has been written on the assumption that the author of Colossians was not Paul himself, but that he or she was heavily influenced by Paul's thought. The differences in style from Paul's own writings, exhaustively discussed by W. Bujard, are to be set alongside differences in vocabulary and also in thought; the last is only to be expected if Bujard is correct in contrasting the 'associative' ways of thought of the author of Colossians with Paul's way of arguing, for, as he remarks, 'at heart the difference between Paul and the author of Colossians is a difference in thought-structure'.[1] It is true that many, particularly in the British Isles, fight a rearguard action on this question, denying that the case has been conclusively proven that Paul could not have composed Colossians; however, in my judgement, principles of historical criticism forbid that the odds should be thus loaded against one side in favour of a traditional or conservative position; one rather has to weigh the probabilities even-handedly, and for me the balance seems to come down reasonably clearly in favour of another hand than Paul's.

The differences in content between this letter's thought and Paul's have been succinctly set out by E. Lohse in his commentary in the course of an excursus on 'The Letter to the Colossians and Pauline Theology':[2] there is, first of all, the absence of distinctive Pauline terms, even when the subject-matter is

---

[1] *Stilanalytische Untersuchungen zum Kolosserbrief als Beitrag zur Methodik von Sprachvergleichen*, SUNT 11 (Göttingen, Vandenhoeck & Ruprecht, 1973), here p. 129 (the whole argument is summarized in Kiley, *Colossians* (ch. 1 n. 4), pp. 51–9).

[2] *Col.* (ch. 2 n. 10), pp. 177–83 (the account above is based on Lohse, but differs from his in some respects).

similar to themes which Paul handles; nor is there mention of 'righteousness', of 'law' (*nomos*), even though the letter is opposing a legalistic teaching, nor of 'sin' in the singular, and there is little mention of God's Spirit. On the other hand Colossians uses concepts like 'the forgiveness (*aphesis*) of sins' which Paul does not (except in the quotation in Rom. 4.7). Colossians expects 'good works' of Christians, and there is no sign of the Pauline antithesis of 'works' and 'faith' (*pisteuein* does not occur in Colossians). In its (relatively positive) view of Jewish rituals and regulations as a 'shadow', contrasting with the reality that has come with Christ (2.17), Colossians is in some respects closer to the views of the Letter to the Hebrews (cf. 8.5;10.1) than to Paul. In other respects, too, Paul's thought has been reshaped: Paul's view of Christ's death as a triumph over such mythical forces as sin, death and the Law has been replaced by a victory over mythical powers of a different sort, the principalities and authorities of the unseen world. What Paul mentioned in passing (e.g. in Rom. 8.31–9 or 1 Cor. 8.6), the cosmic role of Christ, has now come into the foreground. This role he exercises now, not just at the beginning or the end. Similarly those who are his share his reign now, having already been raised with him, rather than simply living now in the power of Christ's resurrection (Rom. 6.4), looking for their resurrection in the future (Rom. 8.11). The vision of Christians is to be directed, for Colossians, towards the decisive change that has taken place already in baptism and towards the present, heavenly reality (esp. 3.1), rather than being directed towards what is still to happen in the future, when God or Christ will execute judgement and bring all to fulfilment.[3]

Again, whereas Paul speaks of the Church as Christ's body with its many interdependent limbs, including the head (1 Cor. 12.21) or the various parts of the head (1 Cor. 12.16–17, 21), and does so in the context of his practical instructions, the image is now developed in a soteriological context so that Christ is set over the body as its head (cf. esp. Col. 2.19). The

[3] Cf. Müller, *Anfänge* (ch. 2 n. 26), p. 83: for Col. 'the future has no importance in itself. It will reveal the salvation which already exists, even if it is still hidden.'

term 'church', too, has now taken on a truly universal dimension, so that, even if it may still designate the local congregation (4.15–16), yet it clearly also refers to the entire company of believers.

Furthermore, it is true that Paul may speak of sharing in Christ's sufferings, and that for the encouragement and salvation of the Church (2 Cor. 1.5–6), and of carrying about in his body the putting to death of Jesus, so that death is at work in the apostle, but life in his converts (2 Cor. 4.10, 12); yet nothing there really prepares us for the daring and puzzling assertion that he 'fills up what is lacking in Christ's afflictions' for the sake of the Church (Col. 1.24). On the other hand, Colossians has not moved as far in the direction of a fixed church order as have Ephesians and the Pastoral Epistles: teaching and exhortation is the responsibility of all as well as of the apostles (3.16; cf. 1.28). It is Christ Jesus who guides Christians' lives, even if it is in Christ Jesus as taught to them (2.7), rather than 'sound words . . . and . . . teaching' (cf. 1 Tim. 6.3).

'Hope', too, is not so much directed towards the future, but is directed towards that which already exists in heaven and has but to be manifested in the future (3.3–4; cf.1.5). As W. Schenk puts it, there is really no more need for Christ to appear again in transforming, creative power to bring into being that which is new;[4] the new exists already. The future brings nothing 'qualitatively new', but is only the manifestation of that which already exists.[5] 'Hope' is also here not so much the attitude which Christians have as that to which their gaze is directed.

Thus Lohse rightly concludes that 'Pauline theology has undergone a profound change in Col[ossians], which is evident in every section of the letter and has produced new formulations in Christology, ecclesiology, the concept of the apostle, eschatology, and the understanding of baptism.'[6] True, not all these innovations are the work of the author, but some are rather to be attributed to the traditions with which he or she

---

[4] W. Schenk, 'Der Kolosserbrief in der neueren Forschung (1945–1985)', in *ANRW*, 2.25.4 (Berlin/New York, de Gruyter, 1987), pp. 3327–64, here p. 3347.
[5] Merklein, 'Theologie' (ch. 1 n. 18), p. 429.
[6] *Col.* (ch. 2 n. 10), pp. 180–1.

works in addition to those stemming directly from Paul. However, all of these, like the contributions of the author, may have emerged in communities influenced by the apostle's work and teaching.

The recognition that Colossians is not the work of Paul himself has considerable consequences for the interpretation of the thought of the letter: while in the case of each of Paul's letters one can legitimately compare the thought of the other letters (although each must first be allowed to speak for itself), in the case of Colossians one has no other texts to compare. The position is more like that with regard to Hebrews. Probably not even Ephesians is by the same hand, although its evident use of Colossians suggests that it at least shows how one early exegete understood the letter or how he or she felt free to reinterpret it. But what Ephesians has done to Colossians, Colossians has in some measure done to Paul's thought: what it offers is the understanding or reinterpretation of the apostle's thought by one follower of his.

P. Pokorný has made the interesting observation that Philippians may count as 'a theological connecting link between the main Pauline letters and Colossians'.[7] With Colossians it shares the theme of Christ's exaltation and sovereignty over all creation, including the heavenly powers (Phil. 2.9–11), and speaks of a citizenship in heaven which Christians already enjoy, even if it just as clearly speaks of a still future transformation (3.20–1). It is more doubtful whether this similarity combined with further development is adequately explained as a sign that 'the gospel has in the meantime entered the dominantly pagan world'. It was already in that world when the main Pauline letters were written, and the shift is thus more likely due to Colossians being written, as Pokorný himself believes, by another hand than Paul's, a hand guided by a mind perhaps still more steeped in that pagan world than Paul's was. If Philippians is closer in thought to Colossians that may well be because of its relative lateness and may show the increasing influence of that pagan thought-world on Paul himself.

---

[7] *Kol.* (ch. 2 n. 15), p. 10; cf. also pp. 4–5.

The echoes in Colossians of Paul's various letters need not point to its author's composing Colossians on the basis of these letters. Such echoes could also be explained as due to a familiarity with Paul's ways of expression, such as a close companion of his might possess. Equally, care should be exercised in speaking of a 'Pauline school': such a school undoubtedly existed, but it is necessary for its existence neither that its schoolmaster should be already dead nor that it should have to work solely or even primarily with the apostle's literary heritage. (It would, after all, probably be quite a few years before a school in any one centre possessed anything approaching a complete set of Paul's letters despatched to his various churches stretching from Galatia to Rome; we should not imagine that there was a 'school office' where some ancient equivalent of carbon copies might be filed away!)[8] But whether one describes the echoes of Paul's thought as due to 'literary dependence' or not, they still exist. To that extent there should be no hesitation in endorsing Lohse's verdict that 'the author of Col[ossians] was thoroughly acquainted with the principal themes of Pauline theology'. If the author was not sitting with the text of Paul's letters in front of him or her, then it is even easier to see why the letter is not simply a pastiche of quotations, but rather is a fresh application of Pauline theology to a new problem, the challenge presented by the Colossian 'philosophy'.[9]

Colossians is thus, along with Ephesians, which probably makes use of it, an eloquent testimony to one tradition amongst Paul's followers, a tradition that was not marked so much by a concern to 'follow the pattern of sound words' or 'to guard the truth' entrusted to it (cf. 2 Tim. 1.13–14), but rather was prepared to enlarge and expand and modify the apostle's teaching or, using the qualification of Merklein noted earlier, to continue the adaption of Christian tradition in the spirit of the apostle. Above all its concern was to adapt it to meet new circumstances and new challenges – an experiment in the interpretation of the Pauline heritage, as P. Stuhlmacher puts

---

[8] Cf. the critique of a single Pauline school in Müller, *Anfänge* (ch. 2 n. 26), pp. 270–1, 321, 325.

[9] Cf. Lohse, *Col.* (ch. 2 n. 10), p. 182.

it.[10] It was, for instance, prepared to assert that Christians were already in baptism risen with Christ, a belief that comes dangerously close to that condemned in 2 Tim. 2.18, so close that H. Conzelmann suggests that this verse may have been directed against the teaching of Colossians and Ephesians.[11] (Contrast the future 'we shall live with him' of 2.11 with the aorist of Col. 2.13.) Noting such tensions Pokorný and others have spoken of a bifurcation of the Pauline tradition and inheritance, of two differing and at times opposed interpretations of Paul's legacy.[12] Over against the more conservative tradition of the Pastorals stands that stream represented by Ephesians and Colossians, a more speculative, adventurous stream, marked by what P. Vielhauer calls 'an increasing mythologizing of the Pauline "school tradition"'.[13] In its line of development the latter stream draws near to the views on eschatology and the incarnation expressed in the Johannine literature, in addition to the parallels to the Colossian hymn in the Prologue of the Fourth Gospel. But on the other hand Colossians has not advanced so far along its line of development as Ephesians with its 'mystical ecclesiology' and is closer to Paul's own way of thought and argument.[14]

---

[10] Christliche Verantwortung bei Paulus und seinen Schülern', in *EvT* 28 (1968), pp. 165–86, here p. 180.

[11] 'Die Schule des Paulus', in *Theologia Crucis – Signum Crucis: Festschrift für Erich Dinkler zum 70. Geburtstag*, ed. C. Andresen and G. Klein (Tübingen, Mohr, 1979), pp. 85–96, here pp. 90, 93.

[12] Cf. Pokorný, *Kol.* (ch. 2 n. 15), pp. 5–6.

[13] *Geschichte der urchristlichen Literatur: Einleitung in das Neue Testament, die Apokryphen und die Apostolischen Väter* (Berlin/ New York, de Gruyter, 1975), p. 201.

[14] Lähnemann, *Kolosserbrief* (ch. 2 n. 47), p. 163.

CHAPTER 4

# *The continuing influence of Colossians*

In the history of Christian exegesis and thought the chief contribution of Colossians has been exercised through the Christological hymn of 1.15–20. As Gnilka notes, it is significant that two thirds of that section of Schweizer's commentary that deals with 'the impact of Colossians' is concerned with this hymn.[1]

One can readily see the reason for this if one looks beyond the immediate impact of the letter, which Schweizer regards as having its most important result in the writing of Ephesians.[2] For it set the course for early Christians who, like it, utilized the traditions of Jewish wisdom speculation in the development of Christology, but its text, particularly the phrase 'first-born of all creation', became a battleground in the Arian controversy in the fourth century: the Arians argued that 'if [Christ] is first-born of all creation, then obvious he too is a part of creation'.[3] To this the defenders of orthodoxy had to retort, often none too logically, that it meant no such thing, but that the 'first-born' differed in kind from creation. The hymn, and even more the more explicit language of 2.9, also became a *locus classicus* for the doctrine of Christ's two natures, the divine and the human. In the view of W. L. Knox this is hardly surprising: Colossians, in identifying the divine wisdom with Jesus 'as an eternal truth in the realm of metaphysics', 'had committed the Church to the theology of Nicaea'.[4] These

---

[1] *Kol.* (ch. 1 n. 8), p. 77, referring to Schweizer, *Col* (ch. 1 n. 5), pp. 245–89.
[2] *Col.* p. 245.
[3] Athanasius, *Contra Arianos*, 2.63.
[4] *St Paul and the Church of the Gentiles* (Cambridge University Press, 1939), p. 178.

Christological controversies were the chief source of interest in Colossians and have remained so until the present century. However, Gnilka points out that the Colossian hymn became the focus for a somewhat different controversy in the Middle Ages, in the dispute between Duns Scotus and his followers and those of Aquinas over whether Christ's incarnation had only been necessary because of the Fall: the former argued that the world had rather been created from the start in the expectation that the divine *logos* would appear in the flesh as its crown, which would fit in well with a possible interpretation of the *eis auton* of 1.16.[5] That cosmic dimension to the significance of Christ was also developed in the light of the hymn in an influential address to the New Delhi assembly of the World Council of Churches in 1961 by J. A. Sittler.[6] For here, he argues, we see that 'a doctrine of redemption is meaningful only when it swings within the larger orbit of a doctrine of creation', and doctrines of redemption that are content with a narrower scope than the farthest horizons of human experience and of our human environment are inadequate. He laments that in this matter 'the address of Christian thought is most weak precisely where man's ache is most strong', an ache which has grown all the stronger in the more ecologically conscious generation that followed, alerted by an ever rising crescendo of warning signs that this world in which we live is tottering on the brink of collapse. To those at the end of the twentieth century it is even more true than in 1961 that we are faced with 'the care of the earth, the realm of nature as a theatre of grace, the ordering of the thick, material procedures that make available to or deprive men of bread and peace'. Can we develop a Christology that enables us to see these as 'christological obediences' as well as just 'practical necessities'?

But the theme of the 'cosmic Christ' has perhaps been replaced by another phrase as a focus of ecumenical discussion

---

[5] *Kol.* (ch. 1 n. 8), p. 81.

[6] 'Called to Unity', in *Ecumenical Review*, 14 (1961–2), pp. 177–87; it was also prominent in A. D. Galloway, *The Cosmic Christ* (London, Nisbet, 1951), to which Sittler refers. Use is also made of the cosmic Christology of Col. in a rather different way by P. Teilhard de Chardin: see, e.g., his *Science and Christ* (London, Collins, 1968), pp. 54–5.

and reflection today, that of the '*integrity of creation*'; yet again Colossians has, perhaps of all the New Testament writings, the strongest claim to be heard on this theme. But, perhaps disconcertingly, it is the Christological hymn which the author quotes, with its vision of all things reconciled by the work of Christ and under his cosmic lordship, which offers the most fruitful starting-point for handling this theme, rather than the ideas of the actual author, who is more concerned about the redemption of humanity. To that extent Schillebeeckx is correct to say that 'Colossians does not have a cosmic theology'.[7] If the writer of Colossians is concerned with the inanimate parts of the world it is with their effect on human beings. Christ has, as L. Hartman puts it, changed the situation of the heavenly bodies in the sense that we can know that they are subservient to Christ,[8] and so we need no longer fear them or revere them. It is the original hymn which includes the claim that 'in him [Christ] all things hold together', and one could not ask for a much better starting-point for Christian reflection on the 'integrity of creation'. Moreover, if it is unlikely that the author of Colossians made use and appealed to the authority of a hymn of which he or she disapproved, then the fact that it was used, however modified, in itself commends it to our further reflection.

So it is rather the precursors of the author of Colossians who seem to have made the bold attempt to claim for Christ the role of wisdom or the *logos* in the whole of creation, a role in some respects akin to that of the impersonal Stoic *logos* permeating the universe and responsible for its reason and rationality (somewhat as nowadays we regard the universe as structured around mathematical formulae?)[9] But it is one thing to claim that role for a concept like God's wisdom, quite another to ascribe it to a particular individual person like Christ. Still, although the author of Colossians was seemingly not interested in developing this line of thought, it is surely a valid concern to ask about the relationship between Christ and the entirety of creation.

[7] *Christ* (ch. 1 no. 41), p. 187.
[8] 'Reconciliation' (ch. 1 n. 16), p. 120.
[9] Cf., e.g. Davies, *God* (ch. 2 n. 2), pp. 218–23.

And yet can we, with our vastly expanded view of the universe, really make any such claims as the hymn makes? Surely we cannot claim that a person born millions of years even after this tiny corner of the universe which we call the earth came into being was the one through whom all things came into being, who sustains it in being, and is its destiny and goal? Perhaps we cannot do so in the same terms as were meaningful in the first century. But, if it is indeed the case that in this individual we have an insight into the true nature and purposes of the Being who is the source and ground of this universe, however vast it may be, then we too are called to say in terms of our own century what this insight means for our understanding, not just of ourselves, but also of the world in which we live. The language and ideas may be very different from those of those first-century Christians, but the purpose of, and the justification for, what we have to do may not be that dissimilar to the reasons that impelled them. Col. 1.15–20 challenges us to meet this demand as courageously, and hopefully persuasively, for our day as it did for its. We need to do our hermeneutical work anew, and cannot rest upon the hermeneutics of the first century. We need in our day to seek, if possible, to hold together a God who is 'big' enough to be the God of a universe as vast as we now know it to be, and at the same time a God who is personal enough to be the 'Father' whom Jesus trusted, in the conviction that a sub-personal God does justice neither to the experience of Jesus nor to our own experience of the worth and richness of human personality. We cannot give up the cosmic scope of theology, nor should we lightly surrender the vision which Jesus offers of a God who can also love and care for each of us as well as for our world.

Schweizer here lays stress on the distinction 'between the language of worship and the language of doctrine'; for the former includes 'expressions which come alive only as they are experienced in the praise offered for what has been freely given; they cannot be encased in an objective doctrine valid for all time'.[10] Yet, true as this may be, it is still incumbent upon

---

[10] *Col.* (ch. 1 n. 5), pp. 299–300.

the theologian to ask what there is about Christ as seen today
which would justify believers echoing such a hymn of praise to
Christ as we find in Col. 1: can they believe such things about
him as would enable them with a clear conscience to praise him
in such terms? Can they do so without the uneasy feeling that
they are going 'over the top', indulging in an unwarranted
degree of hyperbole and exaggeration, making claims for
Christ which exceeded anything that could be coolly and
rationally claimed for him? If the hymn 'actually says that we
cannot understand creation nor God as its creator without
Christ'[11] what is it about Christ that makes him so indispensable? No doctrine, no form of words, can be 'valid for all time',
but what words fit our situation today?

Yet we have to remember here, too, that the author of
Colossians was apparently not disposed to follow up this particular line of enquiry: he or she concentrated rather on the
implications of Christ for humanity. Moreover the author
stresses not the glories of the pre-existent Christ and his role in
creation, but, however awkwardly, inserts a reference to the
crucified Jesus (1.20). It is in keeping with this that Schweizer
stresses how the author of Colossians speaks of the gospel
preached in all of creation under heaven (1.23)[12] and that
Pokorný goes further and asserts that 'the real form of Christ's
lordship over all is the preaching of the gospel'.[13] Yet at the
same time this preached gospel touches not only our inner
being, but affects our attitude and relation to our world,
animate and inanimate. We cannot therefore limit the scope of
Christ's relevance and redemption to humanity as the author
of Colossians at times does, but we also have to be able to say
how the Christ whom we preach affects that world, and how
our vision of this whole world is altered by our beliefs about
Jesus who is the Christ. If we too are called to 'seek the things
that are above' (3.1) it is not in the sense of turning our eyes
away from this world and ignoring it, but in the sense of seeing
this world in the perspective offered by a Christ who, if he has

---

[11] Schweizer, 'Christ' (ch. 1 n. 7), p. 456.
[12] Ibid., p. 461.
[13] *Kol.* (ch. 2 n. 15), p. 173.

not altered this world objectively, has at least altered the way in which we should regard it, by offering us a glimpse of the nature and purposes of the one who undergirds this world. Our concerns and responsibilities for this world in Christ's name are not just for humanity, let alone people as isolated individuals ('souls' to be won), but for all of the entire cosmos which we can in any way influence or affect.

In part connected with an increased awareness of the crises of our world, political, economic and ecological, has come an increased interest in what the New Testament, and Colossians in particular, says about the *'powers'* that control human life and Christ's conquest of them. It would be easy simply to identify these 'powers' with those 'powers' that we see controlling our human life today, be they social, economic, political or the like. There is the danger even of 'demonizing' the latter so that the analogy with the thought of Colossians becomes closer. That has the merit of stressing the powerfulness of the 'powers' and their elusive all-pervasiveness and that they are greater than the individual person, but surely at the risk of making them seem other-worldly and, worse still, outside our responsibility. For we do indeed know of powers that control our lives, that are greater than us, that seem to take on a life of their own that passes out of our control. We stand and wring our hands, as we gaze at the seemingly insoluble problems of trouble spots like Northern Ireland or the Lebanon, at the legacies of history that bedevil these situations and the legacies of mistrust and the tyranny of self-interest that sets East against West, North against South, black against white, at the unfolding of environmental catastrophe after environmental catastrophe, leaving us wondering what else will come from the Pandora's box that we have opened in the name of civilization and progress. Yet all these forces are this-worldly; they are, moreover, largely set in motion by people like ourselves, and their effects can be off-set, if not altogether stopped or removed, by people like ourselves, if, in responsible and wise obedience to a better vision, we set ourselves to work out the will of this world's God. At the same time, that these forces are 'this-worldly' does not mean that they are wholly visible or material; so W. Wink refers to their 'inner spirituality or interiority', that 'inner, invisible spirit that provides [any power] legitimacy, compliance, credibility, and clout'.[14]

We need to note here that Colossians also provides us with a warning against a one-sided denunciation of these powers, for the Colossian hymn insists that all powers controlling human life have been created through Christ and for Christ. They have a positive part to play, a positive role that they can play, even if they have been perverted into agents of oppression. In the last analysis there is no Gnostic flight from the world, no writing it off here. The world in its totality belongs to God and to Christ, and it should and can serve the divine purpose.

But if an explanation is then sought as to why Christ should be thought to provide an answer to these this-worldly powers, then it is perhaps dangerous to concentrate on the exalted Christ, as is done in Colossians. Admittedly the letter stresses that the exalted Christ has won his way to his exalted position *via* the cross, but it would surely be truer to the deepest insights of Paul to stress rather more than Colossians does the earthly Jesus who was himself exposed to these this-worldly powers (and 1 Cor. 2.8 probably refers primarily to this-worldly rulers, even if Paul sees them as at the same time instruments of supra-terrestrial powers). It is true that the overcoming of these this-worldly powers does not become fully clear until we see that this earthly Christ has been exalted through resurrection, and lives on in the lives of his followers who share his path of frail and apparently hopeless exposure to the powers of this world. Yet both Christ and those of his followers who tread his path, which is an abnegation of power-seeking as the world knows it, manifest already in their lives their victory over the world and its forces, however paradoxical this may seem, by normal human standards. Amidst apparent impotence and defeat they display that in their lives there is a greater power, a humanly powerless power, at work which means life for the world, for it sets its face against the aggressive, competitive,

---

[14] *Unmasking the Powers: the Invisible Forces That Determine Human Existence* (Philadelphia, Fortress, 1986), p. 4.

destructive powers that dominate and blight human life and the world in which we exist.

Thus Colossians provides an evocative and provocative starting-point for Christian reflection on some of the most pressing issues, both theological and practical, that cry out for a Christian response in the late twentieth century. Its answers, however, cannot be our answers, but only a first step towards them. We have to learn from its boldness and willingness to press various traditions into the service of its interpretation of the Christian gospel, and to refashion them for its purposes, to meet the needs of its day. Yet its answers are for its day, not ours, and we stand rebuked by its inventive boldness if we shrink back from using it in turn, as part of the tradition which we have inherited, just as freely and creatively as it used those which it received; we may even need to recapture too some of the scope of the vision of Christ held by the precursors of Colossians, to reclaim something of that broader horizon that was restricted and curbed by the more limited needs and horizons of the writer of the letter, since our service of the gospel and the world demands answers to cosmic questions.

*The theology of Ephesians*

Andrew T. Lincoln

# CHAPTER 5

# *Introduction*

Despite the agreed aims and standardized format for this series on the theology of the New Testament, in which each volume first describes the theology of a document and then also engages theologically with what has been described, it will inevitably be the case that each contributor brings his or her own assumptions to the task. The complex theoretical questions which surround pursuing and presenting a New Testament theology cannot be addressed here, but it may well be helpful to the readers of this particular presentation to be informed briefly how its writer has approached his task.

This particular writer has recently completed a major full-length commentary on Ephesians and has been glad to have been given the opportunity to reflect on the letter's more general theological issues and to provide a more coherent overall account of and interaction with such issues than was possible within the scope of the commentary format. Inevitably, what is presented here is dependent on the previous work, and the indulgence of readers is requested when they are referred to the writer's commentary for justification or fuller discussion of positions taken in the present volume.

Clearly one needs to have some idea of what one is looking for in asking about the theology of Ephesians. What is the theology of this letter? Does it lie in its doctrinal statements and explicit statements of belief, such as those found in 4.4–6? Or since it is a religious document, are all its ideas theology? But simply to talk of ideas may well be too abstract anyway. How does one do justice to the fact that the reflections in the letter are shaped and conditioned by the experiences, individual and communal, and by the contexts, cultural and social, of its writer and readers? In any case, this is a document that is not primarily interested in setting out coherent ideas. It is a letter intended to accomplish pastoral purposes in addressing its readers. It achieves these purposes by rhetorical means, by adopting a strategy of persuasion. In his attempt to persuade, the writer constructs a symbolic universe, which the readers are expected to share to a large extent but which is also meant to continue to shape their values, their perception of themselves and their role in the world. It is this world of religious meaning that forms the context of the symbols, concepts and ethos of Ephesians and that, for the purposes of this study, will be taken as providing the 'theology' of Ephesians. This means that, although questions about the letter's perspective on God, Christ, salvation, the Church, ethics will be asked and answered, they will not necessarily provide the determinative structure for the discussion. Rather the attempt will be made to see these issues as part of the letter's overall symbolic universe as that serves the writer's pastoral and rhetorical purposes.

In this way it is hoped to do some justice to the theology of Ephesians in its own right before asking how much of its world of meaning can be appropriated by present day readers. These aspects of the study are not, however, seen as two totally separate stages, but rather as two different goals in enquiry. Inevitably, the dialectic between the past world of the text and the present world of the interpreter is at work in pursuing the first goal just as much as in pursuing the second. Just some of the more obvious of the variety of ways in which this occurs can be mentioned. The methods employed, and therefore also the results produced, in the attempt to lay out the world of the text in its own right come not from that world but from the very different world of contemporary scholarship and are susceptible to change in line with its developments and fashions. The exposition of an ancient text is never exhaustive and the selection of the concerns to be treated must to a greater or lesser extent reflect the predilections, conscious or unconscious, of the interpreter. Even more clearly, the style and mode of presentation of the exposition will be influenced by the analytical and imaginative preferences of the interpreter which in turn have been shaped by his or her own world with its interests and values.

When, in the final chapter, the dialogue between past and present becomes explicit, readers are entitled to know that the questions raised and suggestions made about the appropriation of the theology of Ephesians come from the perspective of one who teaches the New Testament in the context of a secular university but who is also a Christian believer, a member of the Anglican communion, and therefore involved in his own way in the enterprise of relating the Christian gospel to the personal, ecclesiastical, social and global issues of our day. He is all too aware of the limitations of his perspective. He is also aware of the difference there remains between the role of a New Testament scholar who believes his task is not completed without engaging with the religious dimensions of a text and the broader and more demanding work of a contemporary theologian for whom the Biblical tradition is a source, even the normative source, of a viable and coherent present system of convictions.

CHAPTER 6

# The background of the theology of Ephesians

Of all the letters in the Pauline Corpus Ephesians is the most general in its scope, leading one scholar to designate it 'an epistle in search of a life-setting'.[1] Unlike Colossians, in this letter there is no specific false teaching in view, in the light of which the writer develops his own message. In fact, Ephesians is devoid of virtually all reference to particular circumstances which would enable the contemporary reader to reconstruct with any precision the setting of its addressees. As is well known, one cannot even be sure of their geographical location. In all probability, the words 'in Ephesus' were not part of the original text of 1.1 but were inserted later after a collection of Pauline letters had come into being and it was felt necessary to associate a letter, which at this stage had no place name in the address, with a city in which Paul had worked.[2] Not only are there problems about identifying the original readers, but, as we shall discuss below, because of serious doubts about the letter's authenticity, there can be no certainty about who exactly was its author. Rather than attempting the impossible by searching for a specific life-setting, the interpreter of Ephesians would therefore do well to respect the letter's generality and focus on some of its overall features which may be of help

---

[1] Cf. R. P. Martin, 'An Epistle in Search of a Life-Setting', *ExpTim* 79 (1968), pp. 296–302.

[2] For discussions of the possible textual history of 1.1, see especially E. Best, 'Ephesians i.1,' *Text and Interpretation*, ed. E. Best and R. McL. Wilson (Cambridge University Press, 1979), pp. 29–41; E. Best, 'Recipients and Title of the Letter to the Ephesians: Why and When the Designation "Ephesians"?' *ANRW* 2.25.4 (Berlin/New York, de Gruyter, 1987), pp. 3247–79; A. T. Lincoln, *Ephesians* (Dallas, Word, 1990), pp. 1–4.

in sketching the background against which its theology can be appreciated.

### THE RHETORICAL SITUATION OF EPHESIANS

A firm starting point can be found in the assertion that Ephesians is a rhetorical response called forth by its writer's perception of the situation of the addressees and designed to affect that situation. The contemporary interpreter can at least construct from the letter its implied author and readers,[3] pay attention to the persuasive strategies it employs and thereby infer the rhetorical situation to which the letter was meant to be an appropriate response. From there the interpreter can move more tentatively on to less firm terrain and attempt to match the rhetorical situation with an actual historical setting.

The implied author is the apostle Paul who presents himself as a suffering prisoner for Christ on behalf of the Gentiles (cf. 1.1; 3.1,13; 4.1; 6.19,20). He claims he has been given a special revelation about the place of the Gentiles in the Church and asks his readers to recognize his distinctive insight in what he has written (3.2–6; cf. 2.11–22). But he sets himself among other holy apostles and prophets as a recipient of this revelation (3.5) and sees himself with them as part of the foundation of the Church (2.20). Yet at the same time he can describe himself as 'the very least of all the saints' (3.8).

Among the prominent aspects of the implied author's perspective are his appreciation of God's gracious initiative in providing salvation in Christ, a salvation which embraces harmony for the whole cosmos, and his confidence in the power of God to achieve his purposes (cf. especially chapters 1 and 2). He believes that through Christ's work of reconciliation the unity of Jew and Gentile in the Church as a new creation has been achieved and in the process the law has been abolished

---

[3] The terminology of implied author and implied readers is borrowed from literary criticism, cf. e.g. S. Chatman, *Story and Discourse* (Ithaca and London, Cornell University Press, 1978), pp. 147–51. As will become clear, it is particularly appropriate to the initial discussion of Ephesians, where in all probability the name of the implied author is not that of the real author and where there is so little information about actual readers.

(2.11–18). Particularly important for him is the role of the Church in God's purposes and the place of apostles, prophets, evangelists, pastors and teachers in realizing its unity and bringing it to maturity (1.22, 23; 2.19–22; 3.10, 21; 4.1–16). He is also concerned about the way its members conduct themselves in the world, how they speak, their sexual morality, the quality of their worship, their household relationships and their battle against evil cosmic powers (chapters 4–6).

The implied readers are Christian believers, who are seen as having links with all saints (2.19; 3.18; 6.18) and being part of the universal Church (1.22; 3.10,21; 5.23,25,27,29,32). They are Gentile Christians (2.11–13; 3.1; 4.17), who are assumed to know of Paul and his suffering ministry for the gospel (3.1; 6.19, 20) and who have received Christian teaching, including ethical instruction (4.20–4). Despite their experience of God's love and grace in salvation, they are those who need reminding of their privileges (cf. 1.3–14; 2.1–22) and of the debt they owe to Paul's unique ministry (3.1–13). They are also in need of greater insight and further knowledge of all that their salvation entails, particularly of the power of God displayed in Christ's resurrection and exaltation and now available to them (1.17–23). In addition, they need a more complete experience of the presence of the Spirit and of Christ within them, of the love of Christ and of the fullness of the life and power of God (3.14–19).

The picture of the implied readers that emerges from the second half of the letter is of those who, recognizing the special role of their pastors and teachers, are to help the Church to attain to unity and maturity (4.1–16) and to pay special attention to their behaviour in the areas of dealing with anger, edifying speech, forgiveness and love, sexual purity, worship and thanksgiving (4.17–5.20). They need to bring distinctively Christian motivation to their conduct in the household (5.20–6.9) and to resolve to stand firm as they avail themselves of Christ's strength and God's armour in lives of truthfulness, righteousness, peace, faith, prayerfulness and alertness (6.10–20).

In order to meet the perceived needs of his implied readers, the implied author has adopted a twofold strategy which corresponds to the two distinctive parts of his letter. Ephesians replaces the usual body of the Pauline letter by extending both the thanksgiving period and the paraenesis so that these function as the equivalent to the two halves of the body.[4] Within its framework of an extended thanksgiving, the first part of the letter (1.3–3.21) reminds the implied readers of the privileges and status they enjoy as believers in Christ and members of the Church and of their significance in God's plan for his world. It makes use of elements of the Pauline letter form, which also give this half a liturgical flavour, opening with a eulogy or blessing of God (1.3–14), moving to a thanksgiving period with its intercessory prayer-report (1.15–23), and returning to this later (3.1, 14–19) before rounding off with a doxology (3.20, 21). In between the two prayer-reports are elements of anamnesis, the recalling of the past in ways that are formative for the present. There are two contrasts between the implied readers' past and their present (2.1–10; 2.11–22) and then a reminder of what they owe to Paul's ministry (3.2–13). The *parakalō* clause of 4.1 provides the transition to the second part (4.1–6.20), a lengthy ethical exhortation, which calls on them in the light of their privileged position to conduct their lives in an appropriately distinctive fashion in the Church and in the world.

The reminders of the first half in the context of praise and thanksgiving take the form of a celebration before God of all that he has accomplished for the implied readers and can be seen as a Christian version of the ancient letter of congratulation.[5] The second half is a variation of the Greek letter of advice, so that the letter as a whole is a mixed one, combining the congratulatory and the paraenetic types of letter.[6] In terms of a more rhetorical analysis, the discourse of Ephesians combines the epideictic genre in its first half with the deliberative

---

[4] For a discussion and outline of the epistolary and rhetorical analysis of the letter, see Lincoln, *Ephesians*, pp. xxxvi–xliv.

[5] Cf. also N. A. Dahl, 'Interpreting Ephesians: Then and Now', *CurTM* 5 (1978), p. 141.

[6] On these letter types, see A. J. Malherbe, 'Ancient Epistolary Theorists', *Ohio Journal of Religious Studies* 5 (1977), pp. 28–39, 62–77.

in its second.[7] Epideictic discourse attempts to persuade by increasing an audience's allegiance to certain values, while deliberative rhetoric seeks to persuade that audience to take particular actions in the future. The celebration, thanksgiving, prayer and anamnesis of chapters 1–3 serve to consolidate the implied writer's and readers' common relationship to God and Christ and the common values and perspectives entailed in this relationship, and they do this in a way that appeals to the implied readers' religious experience, emotions and commitment. These chapters provide a highly effective springboard for the deliberative argument of the second part of the letter in chapters 4–6, which calls for behaviour in line with the values of those who belong to the Church. The *peroratio*, the concluding summarizing appeal, is particularly important rhetorically. In Ephesians this is found in 6.10–20 with its threefold call to stand firm in the spiritual battle, and, significantly, it combines both epideictic and deliberative features, appealing to the audience both to preserve the status they have been given against all opposition and to demonstrate it in lives of truth, righteousness, peace and faith.

The rhetorical situation of this letter is one in which its implied readers are not as aware as they should be of some key elements of their Christian identity and consequently are also falling short in displaying the conduct appropriate to such an identity. To employ the letter's own terminology, they need to know what is the hope of their calling (cf. 1.18) and to lead lives worthy of the calling with which they have been called (cf. 4.1). Ephesians, then, can be seen as an attempt to reinforce its implied readers' identities as those who have received a salvation which makes them members of the Church and to underscore the necessity of their distinctive role and conduct in the Church and in the world. It can be inferred from the implied author's prayers for them (cf. 1.16*b*–19; 3.14–19) and from his appeals which introduce and conclude the paraenesis (cf. 4.1–16; 6.10–20) that their main problems

---

[7] On the three main categories in ancient rhetoric, see e.g. G. A. Kennedy, *New Testament Interpretation through Rhetorical Criticism* (Chapel Hill and London, University of North Carolina Press, 1984), pp. 19, 20.

accommodating to its values. Hope too of the imminent salvation of all Israel expected by Paul would have begun to fade
with the destruction of Jerusalem, and Gentile Christians in
particular would have needed reminding of the Church's place
in God's purpose in history which had previously included his
election of Israel (cf. 2.11–22).

It is into such a setting of Gentile Christianity in the
churches of the Pauline mission, probably between 80 and 90
CE and possibly in western Asia Minor, that Ephesians aims its
message. It attempts to renew its readers' sense of identity by
reminding them of the privileges of the great salvation which
they have experienced and of their place in the Church with its
highly significant role in God's purposes for the cosmos as a
whole. And it attempts this in order to produce the impetus for
a renewed resolve to preserve the unity of the Church and to
embody the distinctive ethical qualities of the new humanity
they have become in Christ.[14] So, while Ephesians addresses
less specific needs than do the letters of Paul, it does have clear
needs of its readers in view and is not to be designated simply a
theological treatise.[15]

### THE TRADITIONS INCORPORATED INTO THE SYMBOLIC WORLD OF EPHESIANS

In attempting to persuade his readers of his vision of Christian
existence, the writer of Ephesians shows himself to be a creative
interpreter, weaving and adapting into his own world of discourse language and symbols from earlier traditions. One
effective means of reinforcing common values was the use of
liturgical, creedal and paraenetical traditions. Embedded in
the letter can be found not only traditional liturgical forms,

---

[14] Clear evidence is lacking for any of the more specific proposals about the setting of
Ephesians, see Lincoln, *Ephesians*, pp. lxxix–lxxxi.

[15] *Contra* e.g. H. Conzelmann, 'Der Brief an die Epheser', in *Die Briefe an die Galater,
Epheser, Philipper, Kolosser, Thessalonicher und Philemon.* ed. J. Becker, H. Conzelmann
and G. Friedrich. (Göttingen, Vandenhoeck & Ruprecht, 1976), p. 86, who holds
the letter to be a theoretical theological essay; J. C. Beker, *Heirs of Paul* (Minneapolis, Fortress, 1991), pp. 88, 95, who sees it as a compendium of Paul's thought, a
general theological treatise.

giving and worship. As opposed to the direct, incisive argumentation of Paul's letters, Ephesians has many lengthy sentences (cf. 1.3–14; 1.15–23; 2.1–7; 3.1–7; 3.14–19; 4.11–16; 5.7–13; 6.14–20), which extend by means of relative and participial clauses. It strings together prepositional phrases and has a fondness for synonyms, which it links by genitival constructions or piles together for emphasis. Not only the language but also the thought of Ephesians is distinctive. Its focus is not so much on the death of Christ as on his exaltation and cosmic lordship, and there is a corresponding concentration on realized eschatology. Talk of justification and works of the law is absent, and reference to the church is now exclusively to the universal Church.[10] Connected with these changes of emphasis in thought is a perspective which appears to be later than that of Paul. In particular, 2.11–22 reflects none of Paul's struggles over the admission of Gentiles but looks back on an achieved unity of Jews and Gentiles in a new creation with the law abrogated and Israel as an entity in the past. Paul features along with the other apostles and prophets as part of the Church's foundation (2.20). Chapter 3.1–13 also reflects this retrospective estimate of Paul's apostleship on the part of someone who wishes to boost the apostle's authoritative teaching in a later situation.

Most decisive against Paul as author of Ephesians is its dependence on Colossians and its use of other Pauline letters, particularly Romans.[11] Of the 2,411 words in Ephesians 26.5 per cent are paralleled in Colossians and in one passage, the recommendation of Tychicus, there is an extended verbatim agreement of twenty-nine consecutive words. More importantly, much of the thematic material of Ephesians is to be found in Colossians, and in its main blocks this material is in the same sequence. A detailed examination of the similarities and differences in the use of words, phrases and themes

---

[10] For further discussion of the distinctive theological emphases of Ephesians, see chapter 8 below.

[11] For fuller discussion, see, e.g., W. Ochel, *Die Annahme einer Bearbeitung des Kolosser-Briefes im Epheser-Brief* (Würzburg, Konrad Triltsch, 1934); Mitton, *Epistle*, pp. 55–158, 280–338; H. Merklein, *Das kirchliche Amt nach dem Epheserbrief* (Munich, Kösel, 1973), pp. 28–44; Lincoln, *Ephesians*, pp. xlvii–lviii; lxvi–lxviii.

such as a eulogy (1.3–14), intercessory prayers (1.15–23; 3.14–19) and a doxology (3.20, 21), but also hymnic material (2.14–16; 5.14) and creedal and confessional formulations (1.20–3; 4.4–6; 5.2, 25).[16] The 'once ... now' contrast schema from early Christian preaching helps the writer in his own contrasts between the readers' past and present (2.1–10; 2.11–22),[17] while the paraenetical traditions he employs include early Christian catechetical material (e.g. 4.22–4), ethical sentences (cf. 4.25–5.20) and, via Colossians, lists of virtues and vices (4.31, 32; 5.3, 4; 5.9) and the household code (5.21–6.9).[18]

In contrast to Colossians, on which it is based, Ephesians makes quite extensive use of the Old Testament – Ps. 110.1 and Ps. 8.6 in 1.20, 22, Isa. 57.19 in 2.17, Ps. 68.18 in 4.8–10, Zech. 8.16 and Ps. 4.4 in 4.25, 26, Prov. 23.31 in 5.18, Gen. 2.24 in 5.31, 32, Exod. 20.12 in 6.2, 3 and Isa. 11.4, 5; 52.7; 59.17 in 6.14–17. These Old Testament traditions are amongst the various authoritative traditions the writer employs as vehicles in furthering his Christological, ecclesiological and ethical purposes.[19]

Above all, as is indicated by his writing in Paul's name, the writer sees himself as a transmitter and interpreter of Pauline tradition. As we have seen, it is Colossians in particular which provides the model which he adapts to suit his own concerns, but it is impossible to say whether he considered Colossians to have been written by Paul himself or whether, knowing it to have come from a follower of Paul, he treated it as a model of

[16] Cf. also A. C. King, 'Ephesians in the Light of Form Criticism', *ExpTim* 63 (1952), pp. 163–6; J. T. Sanders, 'Hymnic Elements in Ephesians 1–3', *ZNW* 56 (1965), pp. 214–32; M. Barth, 'Traditions in Ephesians', *NTS* 30 (1984), pp. 3–25; H. Merkel, 'Der Epheserbrief in der neueren exegetischen Diskussion', *ANRW* 2.25.4 (Berlin/New York, de Gruyter, 1987), pp. 3222–37.

[17] Cf. P. Tachau, *'Einst' und 'Jetzt' im Neuen Testament* (Göttengen, Vandenhoeck & Ruprecht, 1972), esp. pp. 134–43 and the correctives in Lincoln, *Ephesians*, pp. 86–8, 124–6.

[18] Cf. also J. Gnilka, 'Paränetische Traditionen im Epheserbrief', *Mélanges Bibliques.* FS B. Rigaux. ed. A. Descamps and A. de Hallaux (Gemblous, Duculot, 1970), pp. 397–410.

[19] Cf. A. T. Lincoln, 'The Use of the OT in Ephesians', *JSNT* 14 (1982), pp. 16–57. Beker, *Heirs of Paul*, p. 93, is wrong to place Ephesians among pseudepigraphical Pauline letters which exhibit a 'nearly complete neglect of the Old Testament'.

the sort of writing that could be done in Paul's name. In any case, he omits Colossians' specific interaction with false teaching, but takes up and modifies the rest of its main themes. The writer of Ephesians is so familiar with the language of Colossians that he can conflate terminology from different parts of his model. One striking example is his combination in Eph. 2.11–16 of terminology from Col. 1.21, 22 (estranged, reconciled, body, flesh) with that from Col. 1.15–20 (making peace, the blood of Christ, through the cross) and from Col. 2.11, 14 (circumcision with/without hands, regulations). Particularly important for the symbolic world of Ephesians is the use its writer makes of the cosmic Christology of Colossians, his development of the images of Christ as head and the Church as body, which Colossians had already developed from the undisputed Paulines, his borrowing of its characteristic terms such as *plērōma* (fullness), *mustērion* (mystery) and *oikonomia* (the act or office of administrating), and his deployment of its Christian version of the household code.

Ephesians also makes considerable use of the undisputed Pauline letters.[20] Only a few instances can be mentioned. In the eulogy 1.5, with its notion of predestination and adoption as sons, takes up Rom. 8.29 (cf. Rom. 8.15, 23), and 1.13, 14, which speak of being sealed with the Spirit as a guarantee and link the Spirit with the promise, combine language from 2 Cor. 1.22 and Gal. 3.14. Eph. 2.8, 9 depict salvation as by grace, a gift, by faith, involving no works and no boasting, thereby drawing on Rom. 3.24–8; 4.2, while the 'holy temple' imagery of 2.20–2, with its terminology of growth, building on a foundation and the dwelling of the Spirit is dependent on 1 Cor. 3.6, 9–12, 16. The negative depiction of Gentile living in Eph. 4.17–19 conflates the language of alienation from Col. 1.21 with that of futility of mind, darkened thinking and a giving over to impurity from Rom. 1.21, 24. Later in the paraenesis Eph. 5.8, with its contrast between the children of light and those who belong to the darkness, draws on 1 Thess. 5.5–7, while the battle imagery of 6.14–17 – 'putting on the breast-

---

[20] For a fuller discussion of the evidence, see Mitton, *Epistle*, pp. 98–158, 280–315, 322–38, although not all the examples he offers are equally convincing.

plate' and 'the helmet of salvation' – takes up 1 Thess. 5.8. The writer of Ephesians knows Paul's letters, particularly Romans, well enough to draw on their wording and ideas, to link the language of one letter with that of another, and sometimes to conflate material from an undisputed Pauline letter with that from Colossians in his own interpretation of Paul's gospel. He has Colossians as his model but further 'paulinizes' his own fresh interpretation with phrases and themes from the other Pauline letters.

In the recent history of interpretation of Ephesians there has been much debate over whether its world of thought is indebted to the influence of Gnosticism, the Old Testament, Qumran or Hellenistic Judaism,[21] and sometimes these options have been unnecessarily presented as exclusive alternatives. Despite the influential readings of Ephesians in the light of Gnosticism by Schlier and Käsemann,[22] this perspective must be judged to have been imposed on the text. The features of Ephesians which have been the main candidates for Gnostic interpretation are its realized eschatology, its cosmology, its emphasis on knowledge and wisdom, its head – body, bride – bridegroom imagery and its terminology of fullness, mystery and *aiōn* (age). Putting aside the much disputed question of whether Gnosticism predates Ephesians, all these elements can be far more plausibly explained by influences other than Gnosticism.[23]

The influence of the Qumran literature on Ephesians[24] has been argued for a number of the letter's concepts, such as its contrast between light and darkness, its battle imagery, its depiction of the people of God as a temple, its links between believers on earth and the heavenly realm, and some of its ethical exhortations about anger and speech. If these similari-

---

[21] For a review of this history, see Merkel, 'Epheserbrief', pp. 3176–212.

[22] Cf. e.g. H. Schlier, *Der Brief an die Epheser* (Dusseldorf, Patmos, 1957); E. Käsemann, *Leib und Leib Christi* (Tübingen, Mohr, 1933).

[23] For such explanations, see Lincoln, *Ephesians*, e.g., pp. 30–1; 67–78; 94–5; 105–9; 187–8; 362–3.

[24] Advocated by K. G. Kuhn, 'The Epistle of the Ephesians in the Light of the Qumran Texts', in *Paul and Qumran*, ed. J. Murphy-O'Connor (London, Geoffrey Chapman, 1968), pp. 115–31 and F. Mussner, 'Contributions Made by Qumran to the Understanding of the Epistle to the Ephesians', in *Paul and Qumran*, pp. 159–78.

ties constitute influences, some may have been mediated through Hellenistic Judaism or through Paul. In particular, the elaborate language of worship in the first half of Ephesians, which is reminiscent of the Thanksgiving Hymns from Qumran, is likely to reflect the devotional style of the Hellenistic Jewish synagogue, where Jewish psalms and hymns had already been translated into an equivalent Greek style.[25]

It is highly likely that the cultural milieu of Colossians was a Diaspora Judaism open to the ideas of the surrounding Graeco-Roman world, and, given Ephesians' heavy dependence on the language and symbols of Colossians, it is not surprising that such a Hellenistic Judaism should prove the most plausible background for its own thought. Not only do the cosmological settings against which the interpretation of the gospel is elaborated, the head – body imagery, the terminology of wisdom and fullness, and the household code, all derived from Colossians, have their background in Hellenistic Jewish thought, but also many of the letter's ethical exhortations have their closest parallels in Hellenistic Jewish material such as the Testaments of the Twelve Patriarchs. The writer of Ephesians, then, is at home in the milieu of Hellenistic Judaism and brings to this the distinctive heritage of the Pauline gospel with its strong Old Testament background and its eschatological framework, derived from Jewish apocalypses, a heritage which he has modified but by no means abandoned.

[25] Cf. also van Roon, *Authenticity*, pp. 182–90.

# CHAPTER 7

# The theology of Ephesians

Any arrangement of the thought of Ephesians runs the danger of becoming abstracted from the writer's own way of thinking and mode of expression and of appearing arbitrary. Yet one does not wish, on the other hand, to have the presentation of the writer's thought become a running mini-commentary by simply following the sequence in the text. These two dangers can be mitigated somewhat by making the determinative framework for our own categories what we have seen to be the writer's main concern, namely, the issue of his readers' identity, and by endeavouring to keep in mind constantly the rhetorical means by which he pursues his goal. So this chapter will explore some of the major symbols and themes of the letter in the context of its purpose of strengthening the self-understanding and promoting the distinctive behaviour of its readers as members of the Church in the world. It will recognize that the letter's three major ways of reinforcing its readers' identity – through the language of worship (thanksgiving and prayer), the language of anamnesis (the recall of the past) and the language of paraenesis (ethical exhortation) – are not only vehicles for this writer's theologizing but also significant elements in the symbolic universe he constructs.

## WHO ARE THEY?

In line with the way in which Paul often addressed his converts, this letter opens by designating its readers as '**saints**' or 'holy ones' (1:1). And in line with the overwhelmingly dominant emphasis of the letter as a whole, this term, which derives from Old Testament language about Israel (cf. e.g. LXX Exod. 19.6) and is noticeably not used in the singular to refer to an individual Christian in the Pauline Corpus, already indicates that the writer sees his addressees as those who are set apart by God to be members of a larger grouping, namely God's holy people. The term recurs in all three types of discourse used by the writer. It is part of his prayer in 1:18 that the readers might appreciate the glory of what God has done in entering into possession of his people, thereby reinforcing the immense privilege it is to be among the saints. It is this privileged status that is also underlined in asking the Gentile readers to recall their past in contrast to the present, in which they are no longer homeless and to be thought of as 'outsiders' in relation to Israel but instead now enjoy a sense of belonging, as fellow-citizens with the saints, to all God's people (2:18). The term occurs again in the opening section of paraenesis where it refers to the members of the Church who are to be brought to a state of completion by the ministers of the word Christ has given for this purpose (4.12), and, later, in order to provide ethical motivation, appeal can be made to their status, as the writer speaks of what is 'fitting among saints' (5.3). In other places there is talk of 'all the saints', which reminds the readers of their links with and responsibilities towards not just a local group but the whole people of God. They have already demonstrated their concern for the welfare of other believers beyond their own group (1.15); their comprehension of the all-embracing love of Christ is to be not merely some individual isolated contemplation but the shared insight gained from belonging to the whole community of God's people (3.18); and this sense of belonging to a wider community is to bear fruit in the breadth of their concern in prayer (6.18).

The sense of belonging to a group that extends beyond the local community, is also the effect produced by Ephesians' frequent use of the term *ekklēsia*, '**church**'. In Greek usage the term meant an assembly or gathering, but in the LXX it was the main word employed to translate *qahal* and its reference to the covenant assembly of Israel before Yahweh. Although the term is occasionally used in Paul and then in Colossians to refer to the entire Christian movement, it is Ephesians that makes the major move in this direction. All nine references in the letter are to the universal Church, the Christian community seen in its totality.[1] The first reference in 1.22 dominates the last part of the thanksgiving period and sets the tone in emphasizing the exalted status the readers have as part of the Church, since Christ's supremacy over the cosmos is to be understood as for the benefit of the Church. In 3.10, as part of the reminder about the special revelation given to Paul, the Church is again assigned a highly significant role at the heart of the disclosure of the mystery of God's purpose for the cosmos. It is in fact the means by which God makes known his wisdom to the principalities and authorities. If this were not enough to boost the readers' confidence as members of this Church, then the writer's doxology, which closes the first half of the letter, leaves them in no doubt. In the only doxology in the New Testament to refer to the Church, glory is ascribed to God in the Church (3.21). In this striking formulation the Church is seen as the place of God's glorification, the group within humanity whose existence redounds to God's glory. The remaining uses of the term *ekklēsia* are all clustered together in the paraenesis, where, in his distinctive elaboration on the household code, the writer's view of the relationship between Christ and the Church is made the prototype for his instructions about marriage (5.23, 24, 25, 27, 29, 32).

The Church, of which the readers are a part, is seen as a **new creation**. As they are reminded of their salvation, they are told in 2.10 that they are God's work and have been created for good works through his activity in Christ. When they are actually exhorted to such good works, the readers' perception of themselves as a new creation is again important. In 4.22–4 the instruction they have received is recalled and it is that they should 'put off the old person' and 'put on the new person who is created in God's likeness.' As new people, they are to abandon the old way of life as that attempts to impinge on

---

[1] *Pace* R. Banks, *Paul's Idea of Community* (Exeter, Paternoster, 1980), pp. 44–7, who claims the references are to a heavenly assembly permanently in session.

them and instead appropriate the new identity God has given them. Perhaps the most significant function of the symbol of the new person, however, is its use in the latter half of chapter 2 to express the corporate aspect of the Christian movement and particularly its unity. The Church, to which the Gentile Christian readers now belong, is 'one new person' and through his death Christ is said to have created this one new person in himself (2.15). The corporate new humanity is embraced in Christ's own person, and this notion appears to build on Paul's Adamic Christology with its associated idea of Christ as inclusive representative of the new order, into whom believers are incorporated (cf. 1 Cor. 12.12, 13; 15.22, 45–9; Gal. 3.27, 28; Rom. 12.5; cf. also Col. 3.10, 11). The Church is a new creation which replaces the old order's divided humanity of Jew and Gentile. The new person is not merely an amalgam of elements of the old in which the best of Judaism and the best of Gentile aspirations have been merged. Instead the previous ethnic and religious categories have been transcended. In this way the readers are reminded that the community of which they are a part is a new third entity, in which the fundamental division of the first century world has been overcome and which by its very nature embodies the principle of unity.

The essential **oneness of the Church** is underlined in the surrounding context where Christ is said to have 'made both one' (2.14) and to have reconciled 'both to God in one body' (2.16), so that 'both have access in one Spirit to the Father' (2.18). Later, at the beginning of the paraenesis, the writer's call to maintain unity is undergirded by a series of seven acclamations, which remind the readers of the basic unities on which the existence of the Church depends – one body, one Spirit, one hope, one Lord, one faith, one baptism, one God and Father (4.4–6). The assertion of these unifying realities drives home the sense of cohesion and distinctive identity the writer wants his readers to have as members of the Church.

It is this stress on the Church's unity that provides the key to understanding what has been said in 3.10 about its significant role in the disclosure of God's purpose to the cosmic powers. It is not by its preaching[2] nor by its worship[3] but by its very existence as the one new humanity out of Jews and Gentiles, overcoming the division within the old order, that the Church reveals to the hostile powers that their divisive regime is at an end. It serves as a reminder and pledge of the overcoming of all divisions when the cosmos is restored to harmony in Christ (cf. 1.10).

The writer clearly wants his readers to view themselves as members of the group that embodies God's purpose for the cosmos. His letter helps them to know who they are by indicating **their place in this cosmos**. In Ephesians the cosmos (*ta panta*) has two main parts – heaven and earth (cf. e.g. the formulation in 1.10 – 'to sum up all things [the cosmos] in Christ, things in heaven and things on earth in him'). One distinctive of this letter is that on five occasions it employs the expression *en tois epouraniois*, 'in the heavenlies', in speaking about the former sphere (cf. 1.3; 1.20; 2.6; 3.10; 6.12).[4] In the Old Testament and Judaism heaven as the upper part of the cosmos also stood analogically for the spiritual world above and, beyond that, for the sphere of divine transcendence. This general framework left room for a variety of views about the number of heavens. It is this framework that is reflected in Ephesians. The writer can talk of 'all the heavens' (4.10) without specifying whether he or his readers think of three, seven, ten or more heavens, and he can represent God locally as in heaven (cf. 1.20) but also as supremely transcendent, 'above all', and pervasively immanent, 'through all and in all' (cf. 4.6).

The created spiritual world of heaven is inhabited by both benevolent and malign beings. 'Every family in heaven' in 3.15 refers generally to family groupings of angels, but the references elsewhere in the letter to principalities, powers, authori-

---

[2] *Pace* W. Wink, *Naming the Powers* (Philadelphia, Fortress, 1984), pp. 89–96.

[3] *Pace* N. A. Dahl, 'Das Geheimnis der Kirche nach Eph 3.8–10', in *Zur Auferbauung des Leibes Christi*, ed. E. Schlink and A. Peters (Kassel, Johannes Stauda, 1965), pp. 73–4.

[4] For differing approaches to the meaning of this phrase, see H. Odeberg, *The View of the Universe in the Epistle to the Ephesians* (Lund Universitets Arsskrift, 1934), pp. 12, 13 and A. T. Lincoln, 'A Re-examination of "The Heavenlies" in Ephesians', *NTS* 19 (1973), pp. 468–83.

ties and dominions are more specifically to hostile powers (cf. 1.21; 3.10; 6.12).[5] As in the Old Testament and in Jewish apocalyptic literature, these hostile cosmic powers remain in heaven until the consummation. Prominent in the world-view of Ephesians is also an ultimate personal power of evil behind such spiritual beings, which is designated in 4.27 and 6.11 as the devil, in 6.16 as the evil one and in 2.2 as the ruler of the realm of the air. In this last reference it could well be that 'the air' indicates the lower regions of heaven and therefore emphasizes the proximity of this evil power and its influence (cf. also 2 Enoch 29.4, 5; T. Benj. 3.4; Targum of Job 5.7). The world of the writer and his readers was clearly one inhabited by evil powers opposed to human well-being. It was one in which many were left feeling insecure in the face of such powers and in which mystery religions and magic rites offered ascent to the upper realms of the cosmos and protection from demonic powers.[6] Building on the perspective of Colossians, the writer attempts to show his readers that, as Christian believers who are members of the Church, they are also those who need not feel insecure, unduly threatened or powerless, Instead, he asserts, they are actors in the cosmic drama with a significant part to play.

The readers will understand their true place in the cosmos when they see the significance of what God has done in Christ and understand Christ's place in the cosmos. Ephesians stresses **Christ's exaltation and cosmic lordship**. This note is struck from the start in the language of worship found in the eulogy and the thanksgiving period. The completion of God's purpose is anticipated and the unifying of the cosmos and restoration of its harmony is seen as achieved in Christ (1.10).[7] The inseparable connection between heaven and earth that enables both heavenly and earthly things to be summed up

---

[5] Cf. also Wink, *Naming the Powers*, pp. 50–5, 60–1; C. E. Arnold, *Ephesians: Power and Magic* (Cambridge University Press, 1989), pp. 41–69, 129–34; *pace* W. Carr, *Angels and Principalities* (Cambridge University Press, 1981), pp. 93–111.

[6] These concerns are at work in the syncretistic teaching opposed by Colossians and in its writer's response.

[7] For discussion of the time of the summing up of all things in Christ, see Lincoln, *Ephesians*, pp. 34, 35.

in Christ was accomplished when God exalted Christ to heaven as cosmic Lord. Adapting Paul's use of Ps. 110.1 and Ps. 8.6 from 1 Cor. 15, the writer depicts Christ as the last Adam who already has dominion over the cosmos and supremacy over all hostile powers (1.21, 22a). At the beginning of the paraenesis, in the midrash on Ps. 68.18, there is a reminder of the link between heaven and earth, which Christ has established through his ascent to fill the universe with his rule and through his descent, either in the incarnation or, perhaps more likely, in the Spirit (4.8–10).[8]

The readers are to take their bearings in the cosmos from their relationship to Christ. The very first words of the eulogy make clear that, through their incorporation into Christ, believers, though still on earth, have been linked with the heavenly realm and already enjoy the blessings of that realm (1.3). The most striking assertion of their new position is made in the anamnesis of 2.1–10 where, in contrast to their past under the control of the ruler of the realm of the air and in parallel to what has been said of Christ in 1.20, the readers can be said to have been raised up with Christ and seated with him in the heavenly realms (2.6). They participate in his supremacy over the powers and in his restoration of harmony to the cosmos. They have not thereby been removed from life on earth or from the sphere of conflict, as the writer's closing exhortation will make clear, but, in the continuing fierce battle against the still active evil powers in the heavenly realms, they will be able to stand their ground and resist, because they are fighting from a position of victory (6.10–17).

This symbolic universe of Ephesians is one in which the readers should no longer find any need either to attempt to placate the threatening supernatural powers or to think of themselves as merely one more religious grouping among others in Asia Minor. Their all-important relation to the exalted and cosmic Christ also colours a number of the other main images the writer uses to reinforce their identity. This is true of the dominant image of **the body of Christ**, which

---

[8] For a discussion of the alternatives, see Lincoln, *Ephesians*, pp. 244–7.

occurs ten times in the letter (1.23; 2.16; 3.6; 4.4, 12, 16 (twice); 5.23, 29). Building on Col. 1.18, 24 and 2.19, the writer employs this image of the body to stand for the universal Church. In designating believers as the body *of Christ*, the writer remains dependent on the Pauline usage and its notion of incorporation into Christ with its background in Jewish ideas of representative solidarity. Incorporation into Christ as his body does not mean, however, that the Church is identical with Christ, and throughout the letter the body image is used to help believers to see themselves as a compact whole in relation to the exalted Christ as their head. At the end of the thanksgiving period, when the Church comes to the fore in the writer's thought in 1.22, 23, he asserts that God 'gave him (Christ) as head over all things to the Church, which is his body'. Here Christ's headship is not of the Church but of the cosmos, yet it is noteworthy that it is not the cosmos but the Church which is his body, the special sphere of his presence. The Church's special significance is further enhanced in that the writer takes a confessional formulation about Christ's cosmic lordship and subordinates it to his interest in the Church's welfare by claiming that Christ's supremacy is on behalf of the Church. Later in Ephesians the two separate images of Christ as head and the Church as his body are brought together more closely. The Church as body can be depicted as submitting to and receiving its life from Christ, and Christ's headship is understood in the sense of both rule and determinative source or origin (4.15, 16; 5.23).[9]

Elsewhere the force of the body imagery is to stress that the Church is one and indivisible (cf. 2.16; 3.6; 4.4). Yet the body of Christ is a structured unity that can contain the diversity of the essential contributions of each individual member (cf. 4.7, 16) and the special contributions of the ministers of the word who function as its ligaments, providing connections between the various parts (4.16).[10] In 4.16, therefore, the original

---

[9] On the church as the body of Christ and its relation to its head, see further Lincoln, *Ephesians*, pp. 67–72; R. Schnackenburg, *The Epistle to the Ephesians*, (Edinburgh, Clark, 1991), pp. 298–302.

[10] For this interpretation of the ligaments, see Lincoln, *Ephesians*, pp. 262–3.

both dependent on and united with its head in heaven, is the sphere of his presence and rule on earth and, in its unity of Jew and Gentile, is the paradigm of God's purposes for the cosmos in the face of hostile powers.

### HOW DID THEY COME TO BE?

Frequently in Ephesians the writer reminds his readers of the past, of how their new identity has been brought about. This is particularly clear in the two halves of Ephesians 2 with their contrasts between past and present, but is also the case in the digression of 3.1–13 with its reminder of the debt the readers owe to Paul. This recalling of the past in order to shed light on the present takes place not only through the language of anamnesis but also through the language of worship, both that of the eulogy of 1.3–14, which blesses God for all that he has accomplished for the readers, and that of the thanksgiving period and its intercessory prayer-report in 1.15–23, which also mentions God's past activities in Christ on behalf of the Church. In each case these reminders of God's purposes and acts in history and of the readers' own history are intended to evoke wonder, gratitude and praise in the readers for their present privileges. In the process a picture of the past is constructed, which is essential for the readers' clear understanding of who they now are.

Through the proclamation and teaching of the apostolic tradition, including this pseudonymous letter from a follower of Paul, the readers' most immediate link to the past, as 3.1–13 underlines, is to **Paul's gospel and the apostle himself**. Paul is portrayed as the apostle who suffered and was imprisoned in bringing the gospel to the Gentiles (3.1, 13; 4.1; 3.19, 20). Paul was given insight into the mystery about the one church out of Jew and Gentile and its cosmic significance (3.4–6, 9, 10) and in fact his sufferings in the course of proclaiming this mystery have mediated salvation with its eschatological glory for the readers (3.13). The writer wants his readers to be strongly aware that they are Pauline Christians, and, because of his portrait of Paul, for them to remember their

Pauline analogy involving the interdependence of the parts of an organism is retained, but the writer's emphasis is on the necessity of interdependence for corporate growth rather than on interdependence itself.

The image of the body is brought together with another image for the Church, that of **the bride**, in the extended paraenesis on marriage in 5.21–33, in which the relationship between the heavenly bridegroom, Christ, and his bride, the Church, is made the prototype for human marriage. Taking up the image of the bride both from Old Testament depictions of Jerusalem as Yahweh's bride, especially Ezek. 16.8–14, and from Paul's language about the Corinthian church in 2 Cor. 11.2 and applying it to the universal Church, the writer is able, in the midst of instructions about marriage, to remind the readers once more that, as the Church, they are holy and they are united to the exalted Christ. In 5.25b–27 it is explained that Christ's love for his bride was intended to sanctify her through a washing of water so that he might present her to himself in glory and moral perfection. The language of washing with water evokes not only bridal bath imagery but also, and primarily, the readers' experience of baptism. Then, in 5.31, 32, the writer interprets 'the two shall become one flesh' from Gen. 2.24 as referring to the profound mystery that God has now revealed in Christ, namely, the union between Christ and the Church. In this striking claim, the Church is to be seen as the bride who is not only subordinate to Christ (cf. 5.23, 24) but also intimately one with him. The application of the 'one flesh' marriage union to the present relationship between Christ and the Church makes clear that, for Ephesians, the Church does not become the bride only at the parousia but it is to consider itself as already Christ's bride.[11]

In the passage at the end of the thanksgiving period, in which the first references to the Church are clustered, this Church is said to be not only Christ's body but also his **fullness** (1.23). This depends on translating the difficult Greek clause as 'the fullness of him who fills all things in every way',

---

[11] *Pace* e.g. Barth, *Ephesians*, pp. 628, 669, 678.

taking 'fullness' as a reference to the Church rather than Christ and as having a passive rather than active force, i.e. as meaning 'that which is filled by Christ' rather than 'that which fills Christ'.[12] In this way Christ is said to pervade the cosmos with his sovereign presence and rule, but it is only the Church which can actually be called his fullness. Again the readers are to sense their privileged status. Through its relation to the cosmic Christ, the Church, as his fullness, is the present focus for and medium of that presence, which now fills the cosmos in a hidden way but which will do so openly and completely.

In the Old Testament God's glorious presence which permeated the cosmos was to be found especially in the temple, so it should not be surprising that in Ephesians the Church as the special place of the dynamic fullness of Christ should also be depicted through the symbol of **the temple** (cf. 2.20–2). Although this temple can be called 'a dwelling place of God in the Spirit', it is believers' relation to Christ which is most prominent in the use of the image, for this is 'a holy temple in the Lord' and Christ is depicted as 'the keystone, in whom the whole building, being joined together, grows'. As the exalted Christ he has a unique position in the building as the crowning or top stone of the edifice,[13] but he is also related to the temple as a whole, as its structure coheres in him. In this context of the contrast with their pre-Christian past, the readers are not allowed to miss the force of this symbol. In 2.22 they are directly addressed and told that they are the bricks that are being built together into God's new temple. This takes the place of the Jerusalem temple as the special focus of the presence on earth of the God of heaven. As the community of the Church, through their relation to their top stone, the exalted Christ, and through the presence of the Spirit, the readers, not the Jerusalem temple, form the link between heaven and earth.

Through his temple imagery the writer makes clear that Church's new privileged position owes everything to Chr but he also points out that it owes much to the apostles prophets, who are the foundation upon which the Ge Christian readers have been built into the Church (2.20). this assertion the writer points the readers to the **apos roots** that are essential to their sense of being part o Church. The apostles provided a foundational link wit risen Christ and, together with the prophets, gave founda interpretation of the gospel. Those who have been descri the foundation of the Church are spoken of again as 'th apostles and prophets' (3.5) in the following digression Paul's ministry, which singles out Paul himself as the interpreter of what God has done in Christ, particul including the Gentiles in the Church. Through the s Paul as the recipient of revelation (3.3, 5) and on the ive gracing of his ministry (3.2, 7, 8), the revelat authoritative status of the apostolic tradition is under the beginning of the paraenesis, in 4.11–16, evangelist and teachers are mentioned as bearers and preserve tradition in addition to apostles and prophets, the n the past. In particular, the teachers, amongst whom the writer is to be numbered, form a bridge for th between the apostolic and post-apostolic periods. In ing, preserving and applying the tradition, the mini word are held to be constitutive for the life of th Their importance in the ethical instruction of the underscored in the language of the following peri 'learning Christ' and being 'taught in him, as th Jesus' (4.20, 21). As the Church appropriates its fo receiving teaching in the apostolic tradition, it is sl Christ who is the source of a new way of life.

So how are the readers to see themselves? They of the people God has set apart, the new huma part of the one, holy, catholic (i.e. universal) Church; they are incorporated into Christ as his

---

[12] On these issues, see Schnackenburg, *Ephesians*, pp. 80–3; Lincoln, *Ephesians*, pp. 72–7.

[13] The arguments about whether *akrogoniaios* refers to the foundation stone (cf. e.g. C. L. Mitton, *Ephesians* (NCB London, Oliphants, 1976), pp. 113–14; Schnackenburg, *Ephesians*, pp. 123–4) or the top stone (cf. e.g. Caird, *Paul's Letters from Prison*, p. 61; Barth, *Ephesians*, pp. 271, 317–19) are finely balanced. This writer has given

reasons for preferring the latter option in Lincoln, *Ephesians*, Church as a building, see also Schnackenburg, *Ephesians*, pp. 2

founder will also be to remember their identity as members of the one Church and their role in the cosmic drama.

Although in one sense the readers owe their identity to Paul, in another sense the apostle was only the vehicle for the grace of God, to which they are ultimately indebted. That grace was at work through the gospel which Paul proclaimed (3.6, 7; 6.19) and the readers at various times believed (1.13). As 1.13 also makes clear, the truth of the apostolic message has effected for the readers a rescue from the plight of their previous situation; it is the 'gospel of your salvation'. What is involved in the rescue operation necessary to bring about their new identity is spelled out most distinctively in chapter 2, but elsewhere in the letter there are a number of images and formulations which illuminate this accomplishment. The opening eulogy asserts that in Christ and because of God's lavish grace believers 'have redemption through his blood, the forgiveness of trespasses' (1.7, 8). They have been liberated through Christ's sacrificial death and have had their offences against God cancelled (cf. also 4.32). Christ's costly self-giving in sacrificial death is again presented as the grounds of salvation later in 5.2, 25, when a traditional formula is twice taken up and he is spoken of as having loved and given himself up for believers/the Church. The second of these statements occurs in the development of the relationship between Christ and the Church as the arche-type for human marriage, and in that context Christ is also depicted as 'the Saviour of the body' (5.23), who has cleansed his Church from the moral pollution of sin (5.26).

Above all, it is Ephesians 2 with its contrast schemas and dominant symbols of **salvation and reconciliation** that is intended to shape the way the readers think about their past, so that a particular view of the past will lead to a heightened appreciation of who they now are. The first half of this anam-nesis depicts the Gentile Christian readers' past as a condition of liability to God's wrath, of death and sinfulness, and of bondage to evil cosmic forces and the flesh, and contrasts it with the present as an experience of God's mercy, of new life, and of the heavenly realms through their relationship with Christ (2.1–10). The second half rehearses the past in terms of alienation from Israel and describes the present, by contrast, as belonging to the new people of God consisting of both Jews and Gentiles, to the new humanity created by God's reconciling work in Christ (2.11–22). So a picture of the past and of the change that has taken place is drawn from two perspectives. The former is more general and lends itself to personal application on the part of the readers, while the latter takes up the contrast between past and present in terms of Israel's previous privileged position in God's purposes and is more specifically ecclesiological.

In 2.1–10 the writer, viewing his readers' past from the perspective of their present participation in resurrection life, reminds them that their pre-Christian existence can only be regarded as a state of death. This living death was characterized by trespasses and sins, which had caused death in the first place, and associated with the trespasses and sins were the forces of the world, the devil and the flesh. The readers' sinful actions were in line with the norms of 'this world-age', human existence seen in its spatio-temporal context and viewed as hostile to God. Influencing 'this world-age' and at work through its disobedience was a personal spiritual centre of evil, 'the ruler of the realm of the air'. This perspective on the readers' past which emphasizes their bondage to evil forces is juxtaposed with that which underlines their own responsibility, for they, along with all believers, are said to have been those who at one time chose not to obey and instead gave their consent to the inclinations of the flesh, living life in pursuit of their own ends, and therefore fully deserved God's wrath (2.1–3). The writer then turns to God's decisive action in the past which has reversed his readers' condition. This divine reversal, launched on the basis of his rich mercy and great love, involved making the readers alive with Christ, raising them up and seating them with Christ in the heavenly realms. The readers are reminded that what God did for Christ (cf. 1.19–21) he has done for all believers. What God accomplished for Christ he accomplished for him as representative of a new humanity, seen as included in him, so that believers are to view themselves as participants in the events of Christ's resurrection and exaltation.

Those events changed the power structures in history. The readers are therefore to see themselves as those who have been transferred to the new order of life inaugurated by Christ's resurrection and who share its superiority over the old, experiencing the rule of the age to come and its liberation from the powers (2.4–6). As a result of these past acts, they can identify themselves as those who have been saved. The perfect passive participle in 2.5, 8 is the only instance in the Pauline corpus of the use of the perfect tense of the verb 'to save', and its tense draws attention to the continuing effects of God's past rescue act for the readers' present. Later, in the pericope which closes the paraenesis and sums up some of the letter's main themes, the readers are exhorted to receive from God the helmet of salvation. They are thereby reminded that their ultimate protection against the continuing attacks of evil forces lies in this deliverance which God has already effected for them, the benefits of which they need to appropriate (6.17).

In 2.11–22 the writer, viewing his readers' past from the perspective of their present privileges, reminds them that their pre-Christian existence can only be regarded as a state of severe deprivation in comparison with the status of Israel in God's earlier dealings with humanity. This picture of the past employs categories which draw ethnic distinctions and yet are qualified in such a way as to distance the writer from them and to indicate that they no longer have religious significance (cf. 2.11 – 'you Gentiles in the flesh, who are called the uncircumcision by what is called the circumcision in the flesh, made by hands'). This language may well reflect a Jewish Christian perspective. The writer clearly holds that at one time Israel had real advantages and that his Gentile readers by comparison had no share in Israel's Messiah and were excluded from God's electing purpose for the commonwealth of Israel, from the covenants and the promise. From this vantage point they could be seen as destitute of true hope and the true God (2.12). The reversal of their plight is again said to be on the basis of what God has done in Christ and of believers having been included in him – 'in Christ Jesus' – but this time it is described in terms of Jewish proselytism as 'having come near'

(2.13). Yet, as will become clear later in the passage, this terminology is transformed to mean not membership in the people of Israel but access to God himself and membership in the new community created out of both Jews and Gentiles.

As the writer elaborates the past act of reversal, his emphasis is on Christ as the main actor whose work has made this possible and he provides the only extended reflection on Christ's death in the letter (cf. 'in the blood of Christ' (2.13), 'in his flesh' (2.15), 'through the cross' (2.16)). He applies traditional hymnic material depicting Christ as the embodiment of peace and bringer of reconciliation for a divided cosmos to the situation of a divided humanity.[14] Through his death Christ can be said to have made Jews and Gentiles one by demolishing the dividing wall and source of hostility between them, that is, by abolishing the law and all its regulations. The law could be seen as providing a fence around Israel, protecting it from the impurity of the Gentiles (cf. *Epistle of Aristeas* 139, 142), and, as such, it became a sign of Jewish particularism, which alienated Gentiles and was a cause of hostility. Christ's death terminated the old order dominated by this law and by mutual hostility and introduced in its place a new creation with its 'one new person'. This decisive reversal in history is described through the images of peacemaking and reconciliation and has both horizontal and vertical aspects. On the horizontal level, Christ's death brought peace between the two alienated groups of Jews and Gentiles and was the creative power which reconciled them in the one body of the Church. On the vertical level, Christ's death brought reconciliation of both groups to God, making clear, in a way that the opening part of this section did not, that Israel too was alienated from God and in need of restoration to his favour. The writer can now introduce the Old Testament citation, which his earlier

---

[14] Some interpreters dispute the use of traditional material on the part of the writer and argue that 2.13–18 is simply a Christian midrash on Isa. 57.19 (cf. e.g. P. Stuhlmacher, *Reconciliation, Law and Righteousness* (Philadelphia, Fortress, 1986), pp. 182–200; Schnackenburg, *Ephesians*, pp. 107, 112). For reasons for holding that hymnic material has been adapted in 2.14–16 and for a reconstruction of this material and discussion of its links with Colossians, see Lincoln, *Ephesians*, pp. 126–30.

proselyte terminology recalled, in order to illustrate his perspective on the past. He combines Isa. 57.19 with Isa. 52.7 to indicate that Christ's death was his proclamation of peace with God to both the Gentile readers and to Jews, making possible for both the privilege of access to the Father's presence (2.14–18). Again, it is not surprising that, at the end of the paraenesis, this emphasis reappears in the depiction of the Christian's armour under the imagery of 'feet fitted with the readiness of the gospel of peace'. (6.17). Appropriating and preserving the peace achieved and proclaimed in the gospel is held to be believers' best preparation for combat against the evil spiritual forces intent on producing disharmony and alienation.

Because of the salvation accomplished through Christ's death, the readers now have a past, and, therefore, an identity, which include a **relationship to Israel, the temple, the law and the Jewish Scriptures**. In each case, what appears to be most important for the writer is to underline the discontinuities in the relationship. He wants his readers to be aware that they have become linked to God's larger purposes and that those purposes have their own history, but he is most concerned to reinforce their identity in its own right and to do this he stresses its newness. His Gentile readers' former disadvantages have been reversed, as we have seen, not by their being incorporated into Israel, even into a renewed Israel of Jewish Christians, but by their being made members of a community which is a new creation, transcending the categories of Jew and Gentile. They are to see themselves as bricks in God's new temple which replaces the Jerusalem temple (2.20–2).

This attitude towards Israel and the temple is in line with the writer's perspective on the law. Although he can later make use of the fifth commandment from the decalogue as a tertiary warrant for his ethical admonitions to children (6.2,3), his basic stance is reflected in the assertion that in order to remove the divisiveness produced by the law, Christ abolished 'the law of commandments and regulations' (2.14,15). Torah was a dominant force in the old order not in the new, to which the Gentile Christian readers now belong. As the use of the fifth commandment and of the combination of Isa. 57.19 and 52.7 in this passage (cf. 2.17) suggests, though the law has been abolished, the Jewish Scriptures interpreted in the light of the new situation in Christ, can still speak to the readers. Elsewhere scriptural quotations are taken up directly or indirectly in 1.20, 22; 4.8–10; 4.25, 26; 5.18; 5.31, 32 and 6.14–17. Again, however, as 3.5 makes clear, he sees a discontinuity between the past and the present which highlights his readers' new situation. There he asserts that the mystery that Gentiles would be incorporated into Christ and his body on equal terms with Jewish Christians 'was not made known to people in other generations as it has now been revealed to his holy apostles and to prophets by the Spirit'. Even the writers of the Old Testament were ignorant of the sort of blessing that was to come to the Gentile readers.[15]

The writer's recall of the past and his narration of the salvation God has achieved in contrast to the readers' previous spiritual death and deprivation has been meant to give them an increased appreciation of and thankfulness for their highly privileged present situation. Their own role in what has happened is described primarily in terms of the exercise of **faith**. Indeed, they are addressed in 1.1 not only as those set apart by God but also as those who make a believing response (cf. also 1.13, 15, 19; 3.12). There is one explicit mention of and one clear allusion to **baptism**, the rite of initiation which expresses this believing response and marks the transition to the new community of believers. It is significant that in setting out the fundamental unities at the beginning of the paraenesis the writer juxtaposes faith and baptism (4.5). 'One Lord, one faith, one baptism' could well have been a traditional confessional acclamation which had its origin in a baptismal setting, and here the 'one faith' is likely to have in view the baptismal confession of Jesus as Lord and the 'one baptism' to refer to water baptism as the public confession of the one faith in the one Lord. The other place in the letter where the readers are likely to have understood the wording as a reference to their

---

[15] For further discussion of the writer's use of and perspective on the OT, see Lincoln, 'The Use of the OT in Ephesians', *JSNT* 14 (1982), pp. 16–57.

water baptism is in 5.26, where the writer speaks of Christ cleansing the Church 'by the washing in water through the word'. Elsewhere in the letter there are formulations which may originally have had a baptismal setting, e.g. some of the motifs in the opening eulogy, the contrast schema and the dying and rising language in 2.1–10, the language of putting off and putting on in 4.22–4 and the associated list of vices and virtues in 4.31, 32, and the citation of the early Christian hymnic fragment in 5.14. None of this is sufficient, however, to justify the views of those who wish to argue that a baptismal occasion constitutes the major setting for the letter.[16]

In fact, neither baptism nor the faith-relationship which it expresses are the focus for the writer in his review of the past. In celebrating the change that has taken place for his readers, he diverts attention from their activity to **God's achievement**. Nowhere is this clearer than in 2.8–10. 'For by grace you have been saved through faith; and this is not from yourselves, it is the gift of God; it is not by works, lest anyone should boast. For we are his work, created in Christ Jesus for good works, which God prepared in advance in order that we might live in them.' 'By grace' and 'through faith' are together meant to ensure that the readers will not be tempted to take any credit for their change of status. Faith, in this context, is of course a human activity, but the kind of activity which is a receptive response to the salvation that has been accomplished and which allows it to become operative in one's experience. 'This is not from yourselves, it is the gift of God' is best taken as referring to the whole of the preceding clause[17] and underlines that the whole process of salvation, including even faith as its means, cannot be attributed to any human source or cause but comes freely and undeservedly from God. To prevent his readers falling into any pride or triumphalism, the writer indulges in a double underlining of his point. What has taken place is 'not by works, lest anyone should boast'. In this letter addressed to Gentile

---

[16] *Pace* J. Coutts, 'Ephesians 1:3–14 and 1 Peter 1:3–12', *NTS* 3 (1956–7), pp. 125–7; J. C. Kirby, *Ephesians, Baptism and Pentecost* (London, SPCK, 1968), pp. 144–61.

[17] Cf. also Mitton, *Ephesians*, p. 97; Schnackenburg, *Ephesians*, p. 98; Lincoln, *Ephesians*, pp. 111–12.

Christian readers 'works' refer not to works of the law but to human efforts in general. In regard to their salvation, no activity of theirs can be seen as the ground for boasting. Their privileged position is totally God's gracious work. In fact, believers can be said to have been made by God, to be his work. Everything about their new lives is to be attributed solely to God's grace; even their good works, which they, to be sure, must carry out, can be said to have been prepared by God in advance.

So, in keeping with the response of thanksgiving and praise which he wishes to evoke in the first part of the letter, the writer's emphasis in his depiction of his readers' past falls squarely on God's activity in Christ and particularly on the **divine power and grace** at work in the gospel. It is with his description of God's power that the writer's first intercessory prayer-report begins to digress – 'what is the surpassing greatness of his power toward us who believe, according to the working of his mighty strength' (1.19). He then declares how God has demonstrated that power in raising and exalting Christ, in doing the same for his readers who were spiritually dead (1.20–2.10) and in energizing the ministry of the apostle Paul, who in his gospel proclaimed this accomplishment of God in Christ, especially its effect of including Gentiles in the one new humanity (3.7). He returns to the theme of God's power in the second intercessory prayer-report, asking that the readers may experience that power through the mediation of the Spirit (3.16), and then in the doxology praises the God who possesses this power that is already at work within them, at work in a way that is far in excess of anything they themselves could request in their prayers or even imagine (3.20).[18] The divine grace at work in the readers' past is celebrated not only in 2.8–10, the passage discussed above, but also in the opening eulogy. Indeed, according to 1.6–8, all the blessings of salvation, which the readers have received and for which God is to be blessed, have their origin in God's grace and redound to the glory of that grace.

---

[18] For a fuller discussion of the theme of divine power in the letter, see Arnold, *Ephesians: Power and Magic*, esp. pp. 70–102.

God's gracious initiative is also evident in the disclosures he has made. The readers' lives have been shaped not only by God's powerful activity in Christ but also by his **revelations** about the significance of that activity. The language of 'revelation', 'making known', 'insight' and 'mystery' is found frequently in the letter. 'Mystery' refers to the secret plan of God, which remains hidden and beyond human comprehension, unless he chooses to disclose it. For this writer the mystery which has been made known is the fulfilment of God's plan of salvation in Christ, and various aspects of this plan are unfolded for the readers. Among the blessings of the salvation for which they praise God is the disclosure to them of his purpose for history in the summing up of all things in Christ. The salvation they have experienced in Christ is an all-embracing one which involves the restoration to harmony of the entire cosmos (1.9, 10). The intercessory prayer-report makes clear that the Spirit is available to continue to give them revelation, enabling them to understand the disclosure of God's secret and to live in the light of it (1.17–19).

So far the impression has been given that the disclosures have simply been made directly to the readers, but the digression of 3.1–13 indicates that the primary mediator of the disclosure of God's plan to the readers has been Paul, and, as he passes on Paul's insight, the writer is instrumental in answering his earlier prayer request for the readers in 1.17–19. In two statements, which adapt traditional revelation schemas, Paul's roles as receptor and proclaimer of revelation are underlined. In the first of these statements the radically new insight that has been revealed to the holy apostles and prophets, of whom Paul is *primus inter pares*,[19] is that the Gentiles have become essential and equal members of the new people of God, the body of Christ, an insight that has been displayed in what the writer has written earlier, especially in 2.11–22 (cf. 3.3–6). In the second statement Paul's task is seen as enlightening all people about how God has chosen to work out his secret purpose. This time that wise plan and purpose is said to be

---

[19] In the light of 2.20 and 3.5, this is a more accurate description of Ephesians' portrait of Paul than *solus apostolus*, *pace* Beker, *Heirs of Paul*, p. 71.

revealed to the hostile powers in the heavenly realms and to have its focus in the Church. The one Church out of Jew and Gentile is viewed as a pledge to the powers of the overcoming of their malign rule and of the restoration of unity to the cosmos (cf. 3.9, 10). Later, in his paraenesis about marriage, the aspect of the gospel mystery which the writer chooses to highlight is the union between Christ and the Church. Gen. 2.24 and the marriage relationship of which it speaks point to the secret which has now been revealed, the relationship between Christ and his bride, the Church (cf. 5.32).

Not only is revelation a determinative factor in the Church's formation, but so also are God's **calling and election**. Of course, these notions too highlight God's gracious initiative. The initiative did not lie with the readers; they did not simply decide to believe or volunteer to join the Christian community. What happened to bring about their present status is instead ascribed to God's purposes. In the opening eulogy the variety of terms employed for God's electing purposes is impressive. The passage is pervaded by verbs such as 'chose', 'predestined', 'purposed', 'appointed' and nouns such as 'good pleasure' (*eudokia*), 'will', 'purpose', 'plan', as all the blessings of salvation are traced back to God's sovereign purposes. Indeed, the very first blessing enumerated is that God chose believers in Christ before the foundation of the world to be holy and blameless before him in love (1.4). Believers' sense of participating in Christ, the chosen one (cf. 'the Beloved' in 1.6), is tied up with their sense of being themselves chosen by God, and the language of 'before the foundation of the world' functions to assure the readers that this choice was not dependent on historical contingency or human merit but was rooted deeply and solely in God's sovereign grace.[20] The eulogy goes on to give as further grounds for blessing God not only his choice of believers for lives of holiness and love, but also his predestining them for a relationship of adoptive sonship (1.5). Later, 1.11, 12 underline that it is through believers' relationship to Christ

---

[20] It does not mean that the Church has an 'ontological preexistent status', *pace* Beker, *Heirs of Paul*, pp. 89–90. It is not the Church but the choice of the Church which precedes the foundation of the world, cf. Lincoln, *Ephesians*, pp. 23–4.

that God's choice has fallen on them, and this time their purpose and destiny are said to be for the praise of God's glory. The eulogy of 1.3–14 could not provide a clearer reminder that the ultimate cause and source of the readers' present experience and status is God himself.

It should not be surprising that what has been such a major theme in the opening of the letter is not confined to the eulogy but, in fact, through the related notion of calling, helps to provide an overarching link within the remainder of the letter. God's call is the actualization in history of his electing purpose and in the prayer-report in 1.18 the writer asks that the readers may know the hope that has been opened up for them as a result of this call. The paraenesis of the second part of the letter opens with a heavy stress on this call as cognate noun and verb are combined twice – in 4.1 and 4.4. The readers are exhorted to live worthily of the calling with which they have been called and are reminded that they were called to the one hope of their calling. The use of the language of calling at the beginning of his ethical appeal indicates that, for this writer, God's gracious initiative in election goes hand in hand with human responsibility for living appropriately. If the first part of the letter has set out the high privileges God's call bestows, the second part will set out the correspondingly high responsibilities it entails.

How have the readers come to be what they now are? Again and again the writer's answer has been – through God's gracious initiative effected supremely in Christ but also mediated through his apostle Paul. As the readers come increasingly to share this perspective on their past, it can only evoke gratitude and praise. And, where such an intended response is most apparent, in the opening eulogy, a theocentric pattern to the past emerges. God has acted through Christ for the Church for the praise of his glory. God's gracious purpose has shaped the believing community's past, but because it has shaped the past, it also controls the present and future. Its object is not just to produce a new identity for believers, though of course it accomplishes that, but to bring glory to God himself; hence the variously worded refrain – 'to the praise of the glory of his grace' (1.6), 'for the praise of his glory' (1.12) and 'to the praise of his glory' (1.14).

WHERE ARE THEY GOING?

The writer has described his readers' past in a way that is meant to shape their perception of their present. But the symbolic world of his letter also has a future aspect, which is intended to perform a similar function for the readers, enabling them to understand the present in the light of the future. Not only do the readers need to know who they are if they are to know where they are going, but they also need to know where they are going if they are to have any sense of who they are. Direction and the hope this engenders are essential for their identity as individuals and as a believing community.

But, with his heavy emphasis on 'realized eschatology', is the writer of Ephesians really still concerned about **the future**? One interpreter of the letter has answered this question in the negative and argued instead that Ephesians dismantles temporal categories and projects a world in which time has ceased to be of importance.[21] This is a mistaken interpretation, as we shall discover, but it is easy to see what provoked it. There is certainly no imminent expectation of the parousia of Christ or its accompanying end of history in this letter. Even the statement in 1.10 about the mystery as God's ordering of the culmination of the various eras of history so as to sum up the cosmos in Christ has a present reference. In the context of worship the realization of God's purposes for history and the cosmos can be anticipated and be seen to have been achieved in his exaltation of Christ to heaven as cosmic Lord.[22] But the writer has not lost all realism nor has he discarded all symbols for the future. It is significant that he retains traditional two

---

[21] Cf. A. Lindemann, *Die Aufhebung der Zeit: Geschichtsverständnis und Eschatologie im Epheserbrief* (Gütersloh, Gerd Mohn, 1975). For a full and more balanced discussion of eschatology in Ephesians and its relation to ecclesiology, see H. Lona, *Die Eschatologie im Epheser- und Kolosserbrief* (Würzburg, Echter Verlag, 1984), pp. 241–448.

[22] For further discussion of the temporal reference of this verse, see Lincoln, *Ephesians*, pp. 34–5; Schnackenburg, *Ephesians*, p. 61.

age terminology found in some Jewish apocalypses. In the rhetorical flourish of 1.21 there is explicit mention both of this age and that which is to come (the future age), while in 2.2 the spatial and temporal aspects of present fallen human existence are spoken of as 'this world-age' and in 2.7 the future is seen in terms of a plurality of coming ages.

Other traditional eschatological terms, such as inheritance, kingdom and day, are employed with their usual future connotations. In 1.14 the Spirit is depicted as the down payment and guarantee of a full future salvation, and it is the notion of inheritance which conveys the completion of this salvation in the future. Again in 4.30 it is talk of the Spirit which signals that this writer does have his own 'already/not yet' eschatological perspective and which prompts a reference to the future. The readers are said to have been sealed and protected by the Spirit for the day of redemption, and the term 'day' retains its temporal force as the future goal of history. The future perspective reinforces the present exhortation in this passage. Since the Spirit guarantees their future, believers should be careful not to grieve this Spirit. Later in the paraenesis the future perspective can again provide motivation in the present, as in 6.8 the readers are reminded that, whether they are slave or free, the future day of judgement will bring with it reward for the good deeds they have done.

But there are also negative elements in the picture of the future. In 5.5 the writer reintroduces the notion of inheritance in order to assert that certain people will not have any inheritance in the kingdom of Christ and of God. The kingdom of Christ and the kingdom of God are one and the same kingdom with both present and future aspects, from which fornicators and impure and covetous persons will be excluded. In this writer's perspective the evil days, in the midst of which believers must still live out their lives (cf. 5.16), will culminate in a climactic evil day, when resistance to the forces of evil will be particularly necessary (6.13). The call to stand in the spiritual battle, in which this last reference is situated, itself serves to put the predominantly realized eschatology of the letter in perspective. An eschatological tension clearly remains.

God's purpose of summing up all things in Christ has been achieved in principle and opposing forces have been defeated, but these defeated powers of evil still attempt to thwart the realization of God's purpose. It is because the decisive victory has already been won by God through Christ that the readers are not exhorted to win but to stand, that is, to preserve and maintain what has already been won. The letter's concluding appeal disabuses them of any naïve triumphalism and provides them instead with an optimistic realism about the future.

Further evidence of the writer's concern about the future is provided by the emphasis given to the notions of **growth**, of maturing, of progress towards a goal, and these function as the equivalent in Ephesians to some of the future elements in Paul's eschatology. It becomes clear in his intercessory prayer-reports that the writer is concerned in general terms for his readers' growth. In 1.16b–19 he prays for their growth in knowledge of the hope associated with their call by God, of the wealth of glory involved in God's possession of his people and of the great power available to them, while in 3.14–19 the growth requested is in their knowledge of the love of Christ and their experience of the fullness of the life and power of God. The growth in view, however, is not simply a matter for individuals. When, in 2.21, the Church is seen as the new temple, images of building and organic growth are juxtaposed – 'in whom the whole building being joined together grows into a holy temple in the Lord'. It is the growth of the whole community which is decisive, and the growth is a qualitative rather than a quantitative one, a growth towards holiness.

It is in the reflections on the Church at the beginning of the paraenesis, particularly in 4.11–16, that the notion of growth becomes most prominent. The writer can assert that ministers have been given to the Church to bring the saints to completion (verse 12),[23] and then set out three goals for growth. All believers are to attain to the unity contained in their one faith and one knowledge of the Son of God, to the mature person, reaching a full adulthood which is not individual but corpo-

---

[23] For discussion of the syntax and meaning of this verse, see Lincoln, *Ephesians*, pp. 253–5.

rate. They are to attain to the measure of the stature of the fullness of Christ, taking on the mature proportions that befit the Church as the place of Christ's presence and rule (verse 13). Unity, both of faith and knowledge, was previously seen as something already given to the Church; now it can also be regarded as a goal that has not yet been attained. Both the mature person and the fullness of Christ are depictions of the Church in its state of completion. The Church is already a new person in Christ (2.15) and Christ's fullness (1.23); now it is to attain to what in principle it already has in him – maturity and stature. As they help the Church to become completely what it already is, its evangelists, pastors and teachers enable believers to leave behind the immaturity of children and the instability of those tossed to and fro by false teaching (verse 14). The writer then summarizes the process and the goal of growth – 'speaking the truth in love,' believers are 'to grow up in every way to him who is the head, Christ, from whom the whole body ... makes bodily growth ...' (verses 15, 16). The means of growth is believers' proclamation of the truth which is embodied in a life of love. Whereas previously in this passage the goals of growth have been depicted as the Church itself in its state of completion, now Christ becomes the goal, to which believers must increasingly conform. While ecclesiology is his focus in this passage, for this writer it is not the be-all and end-all; it must still be seen and measured in the light of Christology. The Church is not simply left staring at its own reflection but looking to Christ, its head. The writer does take seriously the Church's future in history. It is this that has led to his recognition of the need to supply a vision of its continuing task and goals and of the significance of the concept of growth for such a vision.

What may well be the letter's most dominant symbol associated with the future is **hope**, and the way this symbol is employed indicates that the writer's view of the future is not merely confined to the Church but moves beyond it to the cosmos as a whole. The noun or a verbal cognate appears in all three main types of discourse in the letter – in the language of worship in the eulogy and prayer-report (1.12,18), in the

anamnesis (2.12) and at the beginning of the paraenesis (4.4).
The Gentile readers are depicted as those who at one time were
separated from Christ and from God's promises to Israel and
who were therefore without hope, that is, without true hope
(2.12). This reminder of the past was meant to cause them to
appreciate all the more the hope they now enjoyed. In the
eulogy they can in fact be described as those who have already
hoped in Christ (1.12), where the compound verbal form
intensifies the future element inherent by definition in the verb
'to hope'.[24] The intercessory prayer-report makes clear the
writer's concern that his readers grow in knowledge of the hope
into which God has brought them by his call (1.18). Here the
stress is on that which is hoped for, and that for which believers
hope is the consummation of salvation. In 1.10, as we have seen
earlier, this was described as the summing up of all things in
Christ, a purpose which has already been achieved but is yet to
be completely realized. Such a content to the hope helps to
explain the emphasis on the one hope, to which the readers
have been called, in the series of seven acclamations of oneness
in 4.4–6. The hope set before the readers is a corporate and
public one, the hope of a unified and reconciled cosmos. Earlier
in 3.9, 10 this hope was related to the Church and its unity,
since there the existence of the one Church out of Jew and
Gentile is viewed as God's disclosure to the powers in the
heavenly realms that his plan for cosmic unity in Christ is being
made good. For the writer the one new humanity is God's
pledge that the one hope will be fully realized.[25]

Hope, in giving expectancy, directs and focuses people's
actions, and the writer recognizes that what his readers hope
for will shape their sense of identity and determine their
actions. Stressing the one hope is therefore entirely appropriate
as a means of undergirding the call to maintain unity at the
beginning of the paraenesis. If the readers have as their hope

[24] For discussion of the disputed phrase, see Lincoln, *Ephesians*, pp. 36–7; Schnackenburg, *Ephesians*, pp. 63–4.

[25] *Contra* Beker, *Heirs of Paul*, pp. 89–90, 110, it is simply not the case that in Ephesians
eschatology has become so subordinated to ecclesiology that the Church catholic has
become the final goal of salvation history and displaced the idea of the Church as a
proleptic reality.

final cosmic unity in Christ, this should produce lives geared to maintaining and demonstrating at all costs the proleptic embodiment of this unity in the Church.

## HOW SHOULD THEY THEN LIVE?

The writer's first answer to this question (it is the first issue he addresses in the paraenetical part of the letter) underlines what has just been said about the ethical implications of the one hope. He believes that if his readers are to lead lives that arise out of and correspond to the identity he has been attempting to reinforce for them, they will do all in their power to **express the unity** the Church already possesses. As he himself expresses it, 'I ... exhort you, therefore, to lead a life worthy of the calling with which you were called, ... making every effort to maintain the unity of the Spirit by the bond of peace' (4.1,3). This will in turn mean cultivating the virtues of humility, which springs from a realization of one's own dependence on God's grace and the worth of fellow-believers, of gentleness, which involves a willingness to waive one's own rights in considering the needs of others, and of patience, which makes allowance for the shortcomings and exasperating behaviour of others (cf. 4.2). What this amounts to is nothing less than learning to love – 'bearing with one another in love' (4.2).

Not only is **love** the quality necessary for unity, but it is also the indispensable ingredient if there is to be any corporate growth or building up of the body (4.15a, 16c). The real criterion for any assessment of Church growth will therefore be how far the lives of its members are characterized by love. Indeed, for this writer, love is at the heart of all of Christian existence. It is part of the goal election is intended to achieve in those it embraces – a life before God in love (1.4). In 5.1, 2 the general call to walk or live in love can be seen as summarizing the previous ethical exhortations and more particularly as the embodiment of what it means to imitate God. And, claims the writer, this costly, sacrificial love is to be the distinguishing mark of Christian existence because it was first the distinguishing mark of Christ, who 'loved us and gave himself up for

us'. This theme of human love as a reflection of Christ's love
will be taken up and elaborated in the marriage paraenesis
when the writer calls on husbands to model themselves on
Christ's love for the Church and to exercise the self-giving love
that has as its goal only the welfare of their wives (cf. 5.25, 28,
29, 33).

Christian existence does not merely consist of ethical
activity. It has a depth dimension to it. Here again, for the
writer of Ephesians, love is involved. In his prayer for his
readers he sees love as the soil in which they are to be planted
and as the foundation on which they are to be grounded
(3.17*b*). This love, which is the cohesive principle of the life of
the new age and the wellspring of believers' existence, is both
the love of God embodied in Christ and mediated by the Spirit
and the power within believers that moves them to give themselves to others with no expectation of reward. The writer
wants his readers to grasp in company with the whole Church
and to know personally the all-embracing love of Christ with
its vast dimensions (3.18, 19). In doing so, they will know
themselves as those who have been accepted and affirmed at
the heart of reality. The depth dimension to the lives the
readers are to live has been in view earlier in the second
intercessory prayer-report with its focus on the inner person
and the heart (3.16, 17*a*). At the centre of their personalities
they are to allow space for the Spirit to do his empowering and
energizing work and for Christ's presence and character to
shape their values and their living. With his talk of Christ
dwelling in the heart, the writer clearly encourages the culti-
vation of a personal relationship with Christ. The letter's
closing grace-benediction reinforces this impression when it
confers grace on 'all who love our Lord Jesus Christ' (6.24).

The depth dimension of Christian existence, nowadays frequently termed **spirituality**, has already been seen in 3.16 to
involve the work of the Spirit in the inner person. Later, the
readers' experience of the Spirit is at the centre of the writer's
exhortations about wisdom and worship in 5.15–20. They are
to be filled with the Spirit, that is, to open themselves continually to the Spirit and to allow this Spirit to have full control

of their lives (5.18). As they do so, they will develop the
discernment to recognize what their Lord requires and the
attitude to time that is able to make wise use of the opportuni-
ties it presents for doing good (5.15–17). Not only so, but their
lives will also be characterized by joyful celebration, particularly in their corporate worship, as they address and edify
one another by means of all the types of songs that the Spirit
inspires and as they sing their praise of Christ from the heart
(5.19) Essential to such spirituality is the attitude of thanksgiving inspired by the Spirit, which will not only express itself
in worship but also pervade the whole of the readers' lives
(5.20). The writer had already underlined the profound
importance of thanksgiving in 5.4, where it stands in stark
contrast to the impure speech and idolatry of sexual lust
condemned in the surrounding verses. Instead of the self-
centredness which characterizes sexual impurity, thanksgiving
presupposes that God is at the centre and gladly acknowledges
him as the creator, sustainer and redeemer of all that is. Those
filled with the Spirit will offer up not only thanks and praise
but all types of prayer, for they are to 'pray at all times in the
Spirit through every prayer and petition for all the saints'
(6.18). In dependence on the Spirit, keeping at bay spiritual
complacency and fatigue, the readers are to pray not only for
their own strengthening for the battle but also for the needs of
all believers and for the free and open proclamation of the
apostolic gospel.

Again and again in the letter the writer underlines his
concern for the **holiness** of his readers' lives. He tells them
that the purpose of their election was that they might be holy
and blameless (1.4), that they are growing into a holy temple
in the Lord (2.21), that they have put on the new humanity,
which is characterized by holiness (4.24), and that the goal of
Christ's sacrificial death was the sanctification of his bride, the
Church, whom he has cleansed by washing in water through
the word in order to present her to himself holy and blameless
(5.25–7). The distinctive ethical purity and separation from sin
which should be part of the readers' new identity are illus-
trated in two major overlapping areas – their speech and their

sexual morality. When the readers were urged to do nothing to distress the Spirit (4.30), the context suggests that what was primarily in view was their use of words in a way that would be detrimental to the work of a holy Spirit who binds their community together. Since believers are fellow-members of the body of Christ, lying, anger, unwholesome and destructive words, all of which endanger harmonious relationships, are to be rigorously avoided. It is speech that is truthful, edifying and kind that will enhance mutual trust and a sense of solidarity (cf. 4.25–32). Then in 5.3, 4 (cf. also 5.12) what is appropriate for those called to be holy (cf. 'as befits saints') is avoidance of talk about fornication, of obscenity and of coarse joking about sex. The writer believes that talking about sexual sins will lead to tolerance of their practice and warns his readers that fornicators and impure and covetous persons will not inherit the kingdom and will experience the divine wrath (5.5,6). This sort of sexual immorality may once have characterized the readers' lives (cf. also 4.19), but those who have a new identity as children of light – and light stands for the realm of holiness – cannot become partners with their unbelieving Gentile neighbours in their disobedience and darkness (5.7,8). Their behaviour is to conform to their identity – 'now you are light in the Lord; live as children of light' (5.8). The readers are to live by values that are radically opposed to the sinful values of the surrounding society, yet at the same time their conduct will shine as a beacon to others, exposing the darkness and illuminating how life should be lived. In fact, as they are true to their own distinct identity as the light, so that light, which has the risen Christ as its source, is able to transform the darkness around it, as they themselves once experienced (cf. 5.11–14).

The writer makes clear that the behaviour appropriate to the new humanity is not achieved by total withdrawal from the surrounding society but by living responsibly in the world, in the ordinary structures of human life, as he takes up the form of the **household code** (5.21–6.9). Here he is dependent on Col. 3.18–4.1, which was influenced by a tradition of discussions of household management in Graeco-Roman writings, stemming from Aristotle, which dealt with the three pairs of husband–

wife, parent–children, master–slave relationships and assigned, as one might expect, the authoritative role to the former and the subordinate role to the latter member of each pair. This writer accepts and even reinforces the basic structures of the patriarchal household, but then within them brings to bear Christian motivations of love and service. His unique contributions to early Christian household codes are his exhortation to all the members of the household to submit to one another (5.21), though for him this is quite compatible with the following exhortations for particular subordination, and his extended treatment of the husband–wife relationship which he compares to the relationship between Christ and the Church.[26]

In the marriage paraenesis the writer's creative use of the analogy with Christ and the Church supports first the appeal to wives to submit themselves voluntarily to and to fear their husbands' authoritative and loving headship and then, in the larger section of the passage, to husbands to love their wives with the same care that they expend on themselves and, even more, with the radical sort of love that would be willing to sacrifice their lives for their wives. Through his citation and interpretation of Gen. 2.24 in 5.31, 32 the writer stresses both the union of Christ and the Church and marital unity. In the context of his letter as a whole, union between husband and wife can be seen as part of the expression of the unity of the Church and therefore also as playing its part in acting as the pledge of God's purposes of unity for the cosmos. In contrast to any downplaying of the marital state for ascetic reasons, the paraenesis clearly reveals an attempt to inculcate in the readers an exalted view of marriage. In terms of external roles and duties, the marriages of those readers who tried to live out this writer's ideal would have looked no different from those of the

---

[26] In addition to the treatment and footnotes of Wedderburn, *The Theology of Colossians*, chapter 2, pp. 56–7, for discussions of the household code in the ancient world and of this writer's adaptation of it, see D. L. Balch, 'Household Codes', in *Greco-Roman Literature and the New Testament*, ed. D. E. Aune (Atlanta, Scholars, 1988), pp. 25–50; M. Gielen, *Tradition und Theologie neutestamentlicher Haustafelethik* (Frankfurt, Anton Hain, 1990), pp. 24–103; 204–315; 546–69; Lincoln, *Ephesians*, pp. 355–65; M. Y. MacDonald, *The Pauline Churches* (Cambridge University Press, 1988), pp. 102–22.

majority of people in the Graeco-Roman world, but the practice of mutual submission and the husband's exercise of headship in terms of loving sacrifice would have given the traditional roles a quite different dynamic.[27]

In his advice to masters and slaves about appropriate conduct in 6.5–9, the writer begins in a fashion unprecedented in the traditional discussions of household management by appealing to the slaves directly. He treats them as ethically responsible persons who are as fully members of the Church as their masters. But in line with the expectations of the traditional codes, they are enjoined to obey their masters and to serve with the proper attitudes of fear of their masters' authority, integrity, wholeheartedness, and enthusiasm. Such attitudes, however, are to flow from their ultimate allegiance to Christ and they are reminded that they will be recompensed for their good service by *the* Master at the final judgement. This is followed by a striking note of reciprocity in the call to masters to do the same to slaves as slaves are to do to them. Their attitudes and actions are to be in the light of the relationship to the heavenly Master which they have in common with their slaves. Specifically, this should mean abandoning all attempts to manipulate, humiliate or frighten by threats. The mutual submission called for earlier in 5.21 is effectively reinforced by the reminder that the heavenly Master makes no partial judgements on the basis of social distinctions. Again, this part of the writer's household code, like the earlier sections, both accommodates to and modifies the conventions of the Graeco–Roman patriarchal household. Its ethos is that of 'love–patriarchalism', which allows social differences to stand but transforms the relationships within them through the distinctive motivation that comes from believers' new identity in Christ.[28]

How should the readers then live? The writer's own summa-

---

[27] Cf. also S. F. Miletic, *'One Flesh': Eph. 5.22–24, 5.31: Marriage and the New Creation* (Rome, Pontifical Biblical Institute, 1988), p. 116.

[28] On 'love-patriarchalism' in the early Pauline movement, see G. Theissen, *The Social Setting of Pauline Christianity: Essays on Corinth* (Philadelphia, Fortress, 1982), esp. p. 107.

rizing appeal or *peroratio* in 6.10–20 adds little by way of specific injunctions to what has already been outlined. Instead it calls on the readers to see their attempt to live out their new identity with appropriate conduct as part of the cosmic drama already set out in the letter's symbolic world. More specifically, it reminds them of their role in the drama by asking them to picture it as part of a **cosmic battle**. The writer's concluding appeal under the new imagery of a spiritual battle combines his two major concerns in the earlier part of the letter – about the readers' identity and status and about their corresponding conduct. As regards the former, the readers are to see themselves as the *militia Christi*, as Christian soldiers fitted out in God's full armour and having available to them all the resources of power that God has provided for them through the salvation he has accomplished in Christ, mediated through the gospel and made effective by the Spirit. As regards the latter, the first four items of the armour are virtues they must demonstrate – truthfulness, righteousness or justice, living out the peace produced by the gospel, and faithful reliance on God's resources in Christ.[29] In addition, the readers' truthful and edifying talk, their purity in word and deed, their love, their thanksgiving and worship, their wise and Spirit-filled living in the household, which have been enjoined earlier, are all now to be seen as part of this battle and as all depending on their appropriating the resources of power they have in God and Christ and on their resisting the evil spiritual forces that oppose God's purposes for them. Above all, what is necessary in the battle is to stand. This is stressed three times (cf. verses 11, 13, 14). The first part of the letter treated believers' identity in terms of their status and position and one of the most striking expressions of that position was that they had been seated with Christ in the heavenly realms (cf. 2.6). The second part of the letter treated what it meant to live out such a calling in the world and in its exhortations repeatedly used the verb 'to walk' (cf. 4.1; 4.17; 5.2; 5.8; 5.15). Now the concluding call combines the emphases on sitting and walking in its exhortation to the

---

[29] On the interpretation of the pieces of the armour as including both ethical qualities and soteriological benefits, see Lincoln, *Ephesians*, pp. 447–51.

readers to stand, that is, to maintain and appropriate their position of strength and victory as they live worthily of their calling in this world in the face of the opposition of evil cosmic forces.

CHAPTER 8

# The theology of Ephesians within the Pauline Corpus and the New Testament

Ephesians is both a reinterpretation of the Pauline message for a later situation and a document with its own distinctive place in the New Testament. Inevitably, however, when its thought is compared with that of other sections of the New Testament, because of its place in the Pauline Corpus, the focus is on its relation to the theology of Paul in the undisputed letters.[1] An assessment of this relationship is complicated somewhat by the role of Colossians as an intermediary between Paul and Ephesians. Whether it is held to have been written by Paul himself,[2] or authorized by him during his lifetime,[3] or written by a follower after his death, as has been argued in the first part of this volume,[4] Colossians represents a halfway stage in the development between the undisputed letters and Ephesians. Ephesians extends still further and, in the process, generalizes Colossians' application of the Pauline gospel to cosmological concerns. In its reminder to its readers of their identity as believers, Ephesians builds on Colossians' emphasis on the cosmic Christ and on its imagery of this Christ as head and the universal Church as his body. It amplifies for its own purposes Colossians' initial use of the household code.

---

[1] On the need for both a comparative and a traditio–historical method for interpreting the deutero-Pauline letters, see Beker, *Heirs of Paul*, pp. 12–17.

[2] Cf. e.g. R.P. Martin, *Colossians and Philemon* (London, Oliphants, 1974); P.T. O'Brien, *Colossians, Philemon* (Waco, TX, Word, 1982).

[3] Cf. e.g. E. Schweizer, *The Letter to the Colossians* (London, SPCK, 1982).

[4] Cf. also e.g. E. Lohse, *Colossians and Philemon* (Philadelphia, Fortress, 1971); J. Gnilka, *Der Kolosserbrief* (Freiburg, Herder, 1980).

ESCHATOLOGICAL PERSPECTIVE

Arguably, what gives the thought of Paul its coherence is its reflection on the implications of the death and resurrection of Christ, and on the interplay between these events, within an eschatological framework. Not surprisingly, this determinative structure has not disappeared from the reinterpretation of his thought found in Ephesians. Rather, what gives the theology of Ephesians its distinctiveness are the modifications to and new emphases within such a structure that its writer found it necessary to make in addressing the particular needs of his readers in a post-Pauline setting.

While the 'already' and the 'not yet' of Paul's eschatological perspective are retained, there are crucial shifts of emphasis in Ephesians. As we have seen, there are still significant future elements in its symbolic world,[5] but what is missing is Paul's sense of imminent expectation of the end and, whereas even Colossians speaks of Christ being revealed at the end (cf. 3.4), in Ephesians there is no mention of Christ's parousia.[6] Instead believers are to look forward to a more extended period of existence on this earth, in which the Church is set goals of growth in its quality of life, and they are reminded of the importance for such growth of the Church's apostolic foundation and its teachers who transmit the apostolic tradition. There is also a sense, conveyed through the household code, of the need for believers to adjust to the values of surrounding society while at the same time maintaining a distinctive identity. The undisputed Pauline letters have scarcely anything to say directly about the relation of parents and children, but now the more long-term view makes exhortation about the Christian training of children appropriate, and it is significant that the writer of Ephesians has no difficulty in quoting unaltered in his appeal to children the promise of Exod. 20.12, which holds out the reward of long life on earth. There is an even more significant difference between Ephesians and Paul in the evaluation of marriage. In 1 Cor. 7 Paul makes it clear, because of his imminent expectation of the end and because of

[5] See the discussion in chapter 7, pp. 114–19.
[6] *Pace* Barth, *Ephesians*, pp. 484–96, who attempts to read this into 4.13.

the need to give undivided attention to the Lord, that his preference is that believers, even those who are betrothed, remain single if at all possible and that those who have wives live as though they had none. Ephesians, however, with its different perspective on the Church's stage in history, no longer treats marriage as a second-best option but by relating it so closely to the union between Christ and the Church gives it an exalted status.

Alongside the adjustment to a more extended future horizon, there is a greater stress on realized aspects of eschatology than in the undisputed letters. Whereas in 1 Cor. 4.8 Paul chides the Corinthians for thinking that they have already become kings and in 1 Cor. 6.2, 3 sees the saints' rule and judgement over the world and angels as still future, in Ephesians there is the striking assertion that God has already raised believers with Christ and seated them with him in the heavenly realms in Christ Jesus (2.6). In Col 3.1–3 such a status is still only implicit and hidden, but here the writer boldly claims that his readers already share in Christ's triumph and rule over the hostile cosmic powers. A realized eschatology with its focus on the heavenly dimension can be found in Paul (cf. e.g. Gal. 4.26; 1 Cor. 15.48; 2 Cor. 12.2–4; Phil. 3.20),[7] but not to the same extent as in Ephesians, where from the start of the letter the benefits of the age to come are regarded as having already become a present spiritual and heavenly reality for believers. The opening eulogy blesses God because he 'has blessed us with every spiritual blessing in the heavenly realms in Christ' (1.3).

## CHRISTOLOGY

Corresponding to the predominantly realized eschatology with its links to the heavenly dimension, the emphasis in the Christology of Ephesians is on Christ's exaltation and cosmic lordship. In 1.10 the disclosure of the mystery of God's will involves the summing up of all things in Christ, 'things in

---

[7] Cf. A. T. Lincoln, *Paradise Now and Not Yet* (Cambridge University Press 1981; Grand Rapids, Baker, 1991), *passim*. The sharp contrast drawn by Beker, *Heirs of Paul*, p. 91, between the Jewish temporal–horizontal eschatology of Paul and the Hellenistic spatial–vertical categories of Ephesians and Colossians is therefore misplaced and ignores the spatial–vertical categories of the Jewish apocalypses.

heaven and things on earth in him'. This cosmic Christology
can be understood more fully in the light of what follows in
1.20–3. There the writer takes Ps. 110.1 and Ps. 8.6, which Paul
had employed in 1 Cor. 15.25–7 to speak of Christ's rule at the
end of history, and applies them to Christ's present status as the
last Adam who is already Lord with dominion over the cosmos
– 'he raised him from the dead, and seated him at his right
hand in the heavenly realms far above every principality and
authority and power and dominion and every name that is
named ... And he placed all things under his feet and gave him
as head over all things to the Church, which is his body, the
fullness of him [Christ] who fills all things in every way.' Now it
can be seen that it is God's exaltation of Christ to heaven as
Lord that ensures the inseparable connection between heaven
and earth and enables the writer to speak of the cosmos being
summed up in Christ. The same belief is expressed in 4.8–10,
which concludes with the assertion that Christ 'ascended for
above all the heavens in order that he might fill the cosmos'.
Clearly the writer's main interest is in Christ's resurrection and
exaltation. To be sure, mention of Christ's death is not totally
omitted. There are brief references in the traditional formulations of 1.7; 2.13; 5.2, 25 and some more extended reflection in
2.14–16 where the writer views Christ's death on the cross as
the creative force that has brought into being the one new
humanity in place of the two old entities of Jews and Gentiles.
What is missing in comparison with Paul, however, is any
extended reflection on the death of Christ as the grounds for the
believer's right standing with God and, more importantly, the
dialectical relationship between the cross and resurrection
characteristic of Paul's thought, which particularly comes to
fore in discussions of suffering and which ensures that for him
the believer's experience of the resurrection life of the new age
remains cruciform (cf. e.g. 2 Cor. 4.10, 11; Phil. 3.10).

## SALVATION BY GRACE

Despite these significant shifts in the dynamic of the pattern of
thought between Paul and Ephesians, some scholars have

continued to regard Ephesians, and particularly 2.8–10, as the most effective summary of the essence of Paul's gospel.[8] Yet even here, where the writer speaks of salvation by grace through faith and takes up themes from Rom. 3.24–8 in particular, important differences emerge. Whereas Paul employs the language of grace, faith and works with justification terminology, Ephesians does so in the context of salvation understood in participationist and realized eschatological categories and seen as a transfer from the old order to the new (cf. 2.5–7). Of course, union with Christ in the decisive events of salvation is a major feature of Paul's thought. Yet characteristic of Paul's discussions and missing from Ephesians are the notions of a future sharing of Christ's resurrection life and of that being conditional on a sharing in his death. What is more, Ephesians can speak of salvation in the perfect tense, as completed (2.8). The closest Paul comes to this is in Rom. 8.24 where the aorist passive is used of salvation but in connection with the all-important qualifying phrase 'in hope'. More representative of Paul's usage of justification and salvation vocabulary is Rom. 5.9, where the aorist of the former and the future of the latter term is found – 'having been justified ... we shall be saved'. By employing the more general and inclusive category of salvation and asserting its completion, Ephesians has taken a step away from the undisputed Pauline letters.

Also indicative of this move away from Paul is the statement of 2.9 – 'it is not by works, lest anyone should boast'. Paul's characteristic terminology is 'works of the law' and elsewhere when he simply speaks of 'works', the context makes clear that the law is in view. His discussion is rooted in the context of his conflict with Jewish Christians over the relation of Gentile converts to the requirements of the law. But Ephesians in its message to Gentile Christians has removed the concept from its original polemical setting and given it a far broader reference. The boasting that Paul had associated with reliance on performance of the law's requirements (cf. Rom. 3.27; 4.2, 4) is

---

[8] Cf. e.g. Mitton, *Epistle*, pp. 268–9; *Ephesians*, p. 100. For a fuller discussion of the issues raised, see A. T. Lincoln, 'Ephesians 2.8–10: A Summary of Paul's Gospel?', *CBQ* 45 (1983), pp. 617–30.

now connected with all forms of self-glorification, as 'works' comes to stand in Ephesians for human effort in general. Grace is a dominant emphasis in Paul's exposition of his gospel. In Eph. 2.8–10 that emphasis is intensified and there is a corresponding decrease in the role given to human response to salvation. Naturally, the response of faith is expected, but the whole process of salvation, including faith as its means, is now seen as God's gift (2.8), and, even further, believers' good works are attributed solely to God's grace because he has prepared them in advance (2.10). In Paul's thinking a last judgement is not displaced by justification and he had stressed the necessity of obedience and love for staying in relationship with God through Christ.[9] There is a strong and serious conditional note about the status of believers in passages such as Gal. 5.4; 1 Cor. 9.27; 15.2; Rom. 11.22, and Colossians retains this in Col 1.21–3. But this same kind of conditionality is not found in the paraenesis of Ephesians, where the warnings of 5.5–6 have outsiders primarily in view.

### THE CHURCH

The importance for his readers' identity that the writer of Ephesians attaches to their belonging to the one universal Church has already been discussed. What needs to be noted here is the shift in emphasis from that of the undisputed letters that this entails. Paul had used the term *ekklēsia* most frequently for the actual gathering of local Christians or for the local group which gathered regularly. In a few references, however, he appears to have in view an entity which is broader than the merely local congregation (cf. Gal. 1.13; 1 Cor. 10.32; 12.28; 15.9; Phil. 3.6). Colossians makes clear reference to the Church which consists of all believers in 1.18–24, but retains the local reference in 4.15, 16. What is unique about Ephesians is its exclusive focus on the universal Church in all nine uses of the term *ekklēsia* (cf. 1.22; 3.10, 21; 5.23, 24, 25, 27, 29, 32). There is a corresponding change of reference in the use of a

[9] Cf. e.g. K. P. Donfried, 'Justification and Last Judgment in Paul', *ZNW* 67 (1976), pp. 90–110.

number of symbols for the Church. The symbol of the body
had had a local application in 1 Cor. 12 and Rom. 12, but now,
again via Colossians (cf. 1.18, 24; 3.15), in Ephesians this
becomes the dominant symbol and is employed exclusively of
the universal Church (cf. 1.23; 2.16; 4.4, 12, 16 (twice); 5.23,
30; cf. also 3.6; 4.25). The imagery of the building of the temple
with its foundation had been used by Paul of the Corinthian
church (cf. 1 Cor. 3.9–17; 2 Cor. 6.16), but now in Ephesians
has reference to the universal Church (cf. 2.20–2). Similarly,
the writer of Ephesians adapts Paul's picture of the Corinthian
church being presented as a pure bride of Christ from 2 Cor.
11.2 and applies it to the universal Church in 5.23–32. There
are other places in Ephesians where a symbol which previously
had a Christological referent is now given ecclesiological force.
This occurs with the use of the term 'fullness'. In Colossians
1.19; 2.9 it had been asserted that the fullness of God dwelt in
Christ, but now in Ephesians the Church is described as the
fullness of Christ, an extension of the thought of Col. 2.10,
where, by virtue of their relationship to Christ, in whom the
fullness of deity dwells, believers could also be said to have
been filled. In 1 Cor. 3.10, 11 Paul had asserted strongly that
there could be only one foundation for the church in Corinth –
Jesus Christ. In its use of this imagery in 2.20, however,
Ephesians has the apostles and prophets as the foundation of
the universal Church. Yet the change of imagery involves no
diminishing of Christ's signficance. The apostles and prophets
are foundational, but Christ is now the keystone of the whole
edifice.

### ISRAEL AND THE LAW

There is no escaping the fact that, in regard to the universal
Church's role in God's purposes for the world, the writer of
Ephesians sees it neither as in continuity nor in parallel with an
Israel which still has its own part in God's plan but rather as a
new creation which replaces the ethnic and religious entities of
Israel and the Gentiles. About the destiny of those Jews who do
not believe in Christ and about the future of Israel, he has

nothing explicit to say. As Dahl puts it, 'the author of Ephesians ... failed to show any concern for the relationship of his
audience to contemporary Jews in or outside the church'.[10]
This is, of course, a different perspective from that of Paul in
Rom. 11, where he pictures Gentile Christians as wild olive
branches who have been grafted into the olive tree of Israel
and looks forward to the salvation of all Israel. It has, however,
rather more in common with the logic of Paul's fierce polemic
in Galatians (cf. Gal. 3.28; 4.25–7; 6.15, 16). A somewhat
similar state of affairs can be posited in regard to the treatment
of the law. The writer of Ephesians speaks of Christ 'having
abolished (*katargēsas*) in his flesh ... the law of commandments
and ordinances' (2.15). This wordy formulation is characteristic of the style of the letter, but has in view, despite the
attempts of some interpreters to qualify its forthright assertion,
an abrogation of the law itself with all its regulations. Such an
assertion does not, however, prevent the writer from drawing
on one of the commandments later for tertiary support for his
own paraenesis (cf. 6.2). For Paul too the period of the law had
come to an end (cf. Gal. 2.19; 3.24, 25; Rom. 6.14; 7.4–6; 10.4).
It is in Romans, however, that Paul takes care to guard his
views and in particular in Rom. 3.31 he denies that his teaching abolishes the law – 'Do we then abolish (*katargoumen*) the
law by faith? By no means! We establish the law.' The writer of
Ephesians, addressing Gentile Christians at a later stage, does
not have to tread as delicately as the Paul of Romans and can
speak of the effect of Christ's death on the law in an unqualified
way.

## EPHESIANS AND THE CANONICAL PAUL

Ephesians has been called 'the crown of Paulinism',[11] and also
'the quintessence of Paulinism'.[12] It is not difficult to see why
such assessments have been made, but once it is accepted that

[10] Cf. N. A. Dahl, 'Gentiles, Christians, and Israelites in the Epistle to the Ephesians',
*HTR* 79 (1986), p. 37.

[11] Cf. C. H. Dodd, 'Ephesians', *The Abingdon Bible Commentary*, ed. F. C. Eiselen,
E. Lewis and D. G. Downey (New York, Abingdon, 1928), p. 1224.

[12] Cf. F. F. Bruce, *Paul: Apostle of the Free Spirit* (Exeter, Paternoster, 1977), p. 427.

Ephesians is an actualization of Paul's message for a later situation after the apostle's death with both substantial continuities and significant discontinuities with the genuine Paul, such designations must be regarded as begging too many questions.[13]

Nevertheless the contribution of Ephesians to the canonical Paul is immense. One of the most significant aspects of this contribution has only recently come to light. In their proclamation of justification by grace through faith as at the heart of the Christian message, many Christians have appealed to the Paul of Galatians and Romans. However, by showing that the historical Paul was not attacking works per se but works of the law in the specific context of the conflict over whether Gentiles should be required to be circumcised and observe other legal requirements, the 'new perspective' on Paul, as represented by such scholars as Stendahl,[14] Sanders[15] and Dunn,[16] whether it is entirely right or not, has made such an appeal problematic.[17] The traditional interpretation of Paul, it is claimed, has come about by reading him through the spectacles of Augustine and particularly Luther. What we have seen, however, is that Ephesians has already clearly interpreted Paul in this way by generalizing the discussion of Romans to make it one about salvation by grace as opposed to human effort in general rather than works of the law in particular. So, by moving away from the historical Paul, Ephesians allows a more universal application of justification by faith to be retained for the canonical Paul, whatever the outcome of the continuing debate about the details of exegesis of Galatians and Romans. Well before the time of Augustine, the generalization of justification and the focus on grace have an unmistakable precedent within the New

---

13 Cf. also Beker, *Heirs of Paul*, p. 110.

14 K. Stendahl, *Paul Among Jews and Gentiles* (London, SCM, 1977).

15 E. P. Sanders, *Paul and Palestinian Judaism* (London, SCM, 1977); *Paul, the Law and the Jewish People* (London, SCM, 1985).

16 J. D. G. Dunn, 'The New Perspective on Paul', now in *Jesus, Paul and the Law* (London, SPCK, 1990), pp. 183–206; *Romans* (Dallas, Word, 1988).

17 Cf. the attempt of J. A. Ziesler, himself an advocate of the 'new perspective', to grapple with this issue in 'Justification by Faith in the Light of the "New Perspective" on Paul', *Theology* 94 (1991), pp. 188–94, where he argues that it is primarily on the basis of analogy that an appeal may be made to Paul.

Testament and within the Pauline corpus itself, as Ephesians sees works as human effort and performance which can obscure the gracious activity of God in providing a complete salvation.

We have already observed that the perspective of Ephesians on the relationship of the Church to Israel appears to have more in common with the outlook of Galatians than with that of Romans. This too has its significance for the canonical Paul. It can be argued that the wheel has turned full circle in the development of Pauline thought on this issue. It began in the heated polemic between Paul and Judaizing opponents reflected in Galatians with an emphasis on the discontinuity between Israel and the new situation God had brought about for Christian believers. It moved to a greater stress on continuity and to a future role for Israel in the context of Paul's diplomacy at a crucial stage in his own mission and in the relations between Jewish Christians and Gentile Christians in Rome. It then returned to the greater emphasis on discontinuity in the thinking of Paul's disciple in Ephesians, which reflects a situation where Paul's position on the admission of Gentiles had been established and where there is a detachment from issues of Jewish Christian/Gentile Christian conflict toward the end of the first century. It might still be argued that Romans represents the more mature thinking of the historical Paul, but it would be difficult to claim that Romans should be treated as normative for the canonical Paul, when it is flanked on either side by Galatians and Ephesians, in both of which Israel's role is replaced by that of the new entity, the Church composed of Jews and Gentiles.

Ephesians makes its contribution to the canonical Paul in a number of other ways. As we have seen, it intensifies Paul's emphasis on grace. In its talk of the reconciliation of Gentiles and Jews in one body in 2.16, Ephesians contributes a stress on the horizontal, social dimension to the notion of reconciliation, which it takes up from Paul (cf. Rom. 5.10, 11; 11.15; 2 Cor. 5.18, 19; cf. also Col. 1.20). As we have also seen, Ephesians balances out the perspective of the Pauline corpus on marriage, as its exalted view of the marital state can be set alongside the clear preference of Paul in 1 Cor. 7 for Christians to remain celibate. Colossians had already brought the cosmic role of Christ to the foreground, and now Ephesians has an even more sustained focus on this cosmic Christ. Together with its stress on the exalted Christ, Ephesians draws particular attention to the universal Church, its role in the cosmos and the necessity of its unity. Romans indicates that Paul had been concerned not only about the unity of believers in Rome but also about the unity of Jewish and Gentile Christians on a broader scale, which he hoped would be sealed by the Jerusalem church's acceptance of the collection taken up from the churches of his Gentile mission (cf. 15.25–31). Yet it is Ephesians, via the earlier move in this direction in Colossians, that consistently sees all believers as one entity, to which the terms 'church' and 'body of Christ' apply just as much as they do to local groups, and it is Ephesians that makes awareness of belonging to this one universal Church an essential element in its readers' sense of identity.

### 'EARLY CATHOLICISM'?

The writer of Ephesians clearly has a vision of the Church as one (e.g. 4.4), holy (e.g. 5.26, 27), catholic, i.e. universal (e.g. 1.22,23) and apostolic (e.g. 2.20). He also underlines the significant role of the ministry of evangelists, pastors and teachers in transmitting and applying the apostolic tradition (cf. 4.11, 16 (where the ligaments represent the function of the teaching ministry); 4.20, 21). How far does this reflect what has been called 'early catholicism' and how far, therefore, does Ephesians, even before the later Pastoral epistles, make the canonical Paul responsible for 'early catholicism'? This of course depends on one's definition of the phenomenon. On the definition of Käsemann, whereby 'early catholicism means that transition from earliest Christianity to the so-called ancient Church, which is completed with the disappearance of the imminent expectation ... there is a characteristic movement towards that great Church which understands itself as the *Una Sancta Apostolica*',[18] the answer appears to be clearly in the

---

[18] E. Käsemann, 'Paul and Early Catholicism', in *New Testament Questions of Today* (London, SCM, 1963), p. 237.

affirmative. If, however, one works with Dunn's analysis of 'early catholicism' in terms of the three broad features of the fading of the parousia hope, increasing institutionalization and crystallization of the faith into set forms,[19] a somewhat more nuanced response may be called for in regard to the last two features.

A heavy stress on the sacraments is usually associated with increasing institutionalization, but, as we have seen, while a number of its traditional elements may have had an original baptismal setting, Ephesians contains only two clear references to baptism (cf. 4.5; 5.26). It is certainly indicative of the importance attached to the rite that in the first of these references baptism is regarded as one of the fundamental unities on which the Church is based, yet the letter as a whole is not overly concerned with this sacrament and there is no mention at all of the Lord's Supper.

Käsemann argues that because of the letter's emphasis on the universal Church, Christology has become a function of ecclesiology in Ephesians.[20] But it is clear that, for all the importance he gives to the Church's status and role, in the writer's thought the Church is nothing in itself. It is a special community only because it has the exalted Christ as its head and because his presence fills it. It is not so much that Christology is swallowed up by ecclesiology as that ecclesiology is thoroughly Christological.[21] What is said about the Church depends on what is said about what God has done in Christ, but at the same time what is said about Christ is always related to believers and the Church.

Ephesians 4.11–16 underscores the position of the evangelists, pastors and teachers of the writer's own time by describing them as gifts of the exalted Christ along with the apostles and prophets. There is no talk of ordination to office or legiti-

---

[19] Cf. J. D. G. Dunn, *Unity and Diversity in the New Testament* (London, SCM, 1990²), p. 344, where these features are elaborated.

[20] Cf. E. Käsemann, 'The Theological Problem Presented by the Motif of the Body of Christ', in *Perspectives on Paul* (London, SCM, 1971), p. 120.

[21] Cf. also H. Merklein, 'Paulinische Theologie in der Rezeption des Kolosser- und Epheserbriefes', in *Paulus in den neutestamentlichen Spätschriften*, ed. K. Kertelge (Freiburg, Herder 1981), p. 62.

mation of office by the church, but to all intents and purposes offices are in view, since evangelists, pastors and teachers were so called because they regularly exercised their particular ministries, which would have required acceptance by their churches, and their ministries are seen by the writer as constitutive for the life of the Church.[22] Ephesians 4.1–16 combines, without any sign of tension, both an emphasis on particular ministries and a recognition that every member has an indispensable role in the well-being of the Church (cf. 4.7, 16). The stage of ministry presupposed by this pericope appears to be somewhat more developed than that reflected in the Pauline homologoumena but not as regulated as that of Luke and the Pastorals (cf. Acts 14.23; 20.17, 28; 1 Tim. 3.1, 2, 5; 4.14; 5.17, 19; Tit. 1.5, 7), which led eventually to the monepiscopacy and the threefold order of bishops, presbyters and deacons.

The reason Ephesians attaches such significance to the teaching ministry is that through it can be transmitted the apostolic tradition, which will bring the Church to maturity and maintain its unity over against the effects of false teaching (cf. 4.13, 14). Ethical aspects of this tradition need to be underlined (cf. 4.20–4). Presumably the writer sees himself as a teacher whose adoption of the device of pseudonymity allows him to pass on the Pauline tradition in a persuasive way. The letter employs hymnic and creedal formulations in addition to its use of Colossians and other Pauline letters. Yet none of this could be appropriately described as the crystallization of the faith into set forms. What distinguishes this writer's transmission of the Pauline tradition is its creative updating of that tradition to meet the needs of his readers which have emerged after the death of the apostle. This response to a post-Pauline setting makes that of the Pastorals with their emphasis on the fixed deposit of faith look defensive and uncreative by comparison.

Within the terms of the debate, then, Ephesians must be judged to contain some, but only some, of the elements of 'early catholicism', which were to characterize the 'great church' of

---

[22] See H. Merklein, *Das kirchliche Amt nach dem Epheserbrief* (Munich, Kösel, 1973), pp. 79–80, 348–92 for more extensive discussion.

the second century CE. It occupies a relatively early place in post-Pauline developments. But increasingly problems have been recognized with this debate. The term 'early catholicism' has sometimes taken on pejorative connotations under the influence of Käsemann's negative evaluation of the phenomenon in comparison with the genuine Paul. There has been a false assumption that leadership in the churches at the time of Paul was purely charismatic. More importantly, the debate has often been conducted too much along the lines of varying theologies and has not sufficiently recognized the complexity of social factors in the development of church life. A more satisfactory attempt to provide an investigation of the same issues in the development of the Pauline churches from a sociohistorical perspective has been made by M. Y. MacDonald.[23] By examining attitudes to the world/ethics, ministry, ritual and belief in each case, she sees the letters of the genuine Paul as reflecting community-building institutionalization, Colossians and Ephesians as suggesting community-stabilizing institutionalization and the Pastorals as indicating community-protecting institutionalization. An approach of this kind allows more justice to be done to the continuities and discontinuities between the symbolic world of Ephesians and that of Paul, which have been our concern in the earlier part of this chapter. Many of the modifications arise from the need, perceived by the writer of Ephesians, in the light of the death of the apostle and the delay of the parousia, for Pauline churches to adjust to a more long-term perspective on their life in the world.

The use of the household code in Ephesians is particularly revealing for the writer's attitude to the necessary adjustment. It is an essential part of his overall attempt to help the churches assimilate to life in society while preserving their distinctive identity. The patriarchal structuring of household management, which was seen as crucial for the stability of society, is taken over, but to it the writer brings his Christian vision of relationships. In regard to marriage, his call to mutual submission and his depiction of the husband's exercise of headship

[23] MacDonald, *The Pauline Churches*.

in terms of loving sacrifice give the traditional roles a different dynamic. Nevertheless, while the writer's adaptation of the code would have resulted in gains for some women within marriage, the instructions about subordination would have had implications for the role of women in the general life of the churches and contributed to the identification of positions with any authority as male prerogatives.[24] The results of this tendency can be seen in the Pastorals, where, as the household became the dominant model for the Church, women were excluded from authoritative teaching roles (cf. 1 Tim. 2.18–3.5). Ephesians treats children as those who in their own right have a relation with Christ. It also provides restraints on paternal authority, guarding against its abuse and calling on fathers to provide Christian training. This emphasis is different from that found later in the Pastorals, where children are not addressed and are seen only as the objects of discipline (cf. 1 Tim. 3.4, 5, 12; Tit. 1.6). We have already observed the clear note of reciprocity in the writer's admonitions to masters and slaves (cf. 5.21; 6.9). By the time of the Pastorals, in which the view of the Church and the model of the household and, at the same time, the perspective of church leaders and that of masters of households have become more closely identified, this note is missing, and it is only slaves and not masters who are exhorted about their duties (cf. 1 Tim. 6.1, 2; Tit. 2.9, 10). The inevitable process of adjustment of the Pauline churches to life in society with its necessary increasing institutionalization, which was to have both positive and negative effects, is clearly underway in Ephesians. But equally clearly at this stage the acculturation was not simply a one-way process. The distinctive behaviour called for by Ephesians in regard to life in the household, which was seen as of crucial social and political concern, would have created modifications of and tensions within the dominant ethos of the surrounding world.

[24] Cf. also ibid., pp. 119–20.

# CHAPTER 9

# Critical appropriation of the theology of Ephesians

Ephesians itself can be seen as a skilful and creative appropriation of earlier tradition for its own time and setting. It is an interpretation of Colossians and of the Pauline gospel for a new situation. As such, it offers help to the contemporary interpreter in at least two ways. It already offers some important clues about how the Pauline gospel can be recontextualized in a setting removed from some of the original issues which shaped it and thereby be made more universal in its scope.[1] It also encourages the contemporary interpreter to continue the inevitable hermeneutical process, to take its appropriation of the Pauline tradition and engage in his or her own critical appropriation of the appropriation.

What is involved in critical appropriation of a text? On the one hand, there must be a willingness to accept the invitation of the text to participate in the symbolic world it projects, to be caught up in its vision of Christian existence. On the other hand, for a critical appropriation to take place, there will also be the sort of distancing that has first allowed the text to retain its own identity and otherness and that then allows those who have been caught up in its world to retain their own identity, as they address questions to the text from their own time and place and assess its truth claims from the perspective of the Christian consciousness of contemporary communities of

---

[1] If the result of Ephesians' creative adaptation of Paul is to make his message more universal in its application, this need not necessarily be seen as disqualifying it as a faithful rendering of Paul's thought, because it has abandoned Paul's 'situation-specific hermeneutic'. Indeed, the need for a more general application, which transcends the particularities of Paul's day, can itself constitute the specific situation of later interpreters, *pace* Beker, *Heirs of Paul*, p. 109.

faith.[2] Only a brief attempt to make explicit some elements of both sides of this reader's critical appropriation is possible within the confines of this chapter.

## MODES OF THEOLOGIZING

Not only the content of Ephesians' appropriation of Pauline tradition but also the mode and form of this appropriation may prove instructive to the contemporary interpreter. In line with the strategy of Paul himself, this writer has identified a need in the churches to which he writes, though a more general one than the needs reflected in Paul's own letters, and his interpretation is targeted to that need. It is particularly significant that he has chosen to begin his message, and indeed to frame the whole of the first part of his letter, with the language of worship. As we have seen, this enables him to reinforce the perspectives and values he and his readers already share and in the process to touch and build upon their religious experience and emotions. Just as thanksgiving, prayer and doxology were both a shaping power and an effective mode for this writer's theologizing, they can also function in this way for contemporary reflection on the gospel and its values. There has been some recognition of the potential of the dynamic of praise for the task of theology, not least in giving theology a distinctive shape and purpose,[3] but there is scope for much more exploration. From the perspective of Old Testament studies, W. Brueggemann has called attention to the power of doxology in the encounter with contemporary idolatries and ideologies. In its response to God, he claims, praise is also an assertion of an alternative world. The liturgy sings and proclaims that God reigns, disestablishing worldly powers and exposing their claims to ultimacy and control.[4] Much the same could be said

[2] For a fuller and suggestive treatment of this issue, see S. Schneiders, *The Revelatory Text* (San Francisco, Harper, 1991), esp. pp. 167–78.

[3] Cf. e.g. D. W. Hardy and D. F. Ford, *Jubilate. Theology in Praise* (London, Darton, Longman and Todd, 1984); also G. Wainwright, *Doxology: the Praise of God in Worship, Doctrine and Life* (London, Epworth, 1980).

[4] Cf. W. Brueggemann, *Israel's Praise: Doxology Against Idolatry and Ideology* (Philadelphia, Fortress, 1988).

of Ephesians. As the writer encourages his readers to become caught up in doxology, he is reinforcing for them the Pauline gospel's alternative vision of existence in which Christ has triumphed over the powers and given all necessary resources to the Church. Thereby the menace and claims of this age with its perverted patterns of behaviour and idolatry (cf. 5.5) and its evil forces are relativized, and the readers are enabled by the same Spirit that inspires their praise to live out the liberation that has been won for them by Christ. Theological reflection would also do well to learn to tap the resources of traditional and contemporary hymns and poetry and to include a rhetoric of devotion in its repertoire. It is noticeable that much of what is taken to be hymnic in the Pauline Corpus has a didactic and paraenetic function in its present form and context (e.g. Phil. 2.6–11; Col. 1.15–20; Eph. 5.14; 1 Tim. 3.16). The language of worship still has both an educative and affective force. It is able to touch religious sensibilities and can enable theologizing not only to instruct but also to move and to motivate its audience, as it asserts an alternative world that provides a basis for hope.

Within the worship framework of the first part of the letter, the writer also makes use of anamnesis, calling on his readers in chapter 2 to recall the past in a way that will make them appreciative of and grateful to God for their present status and experience. Remembering the past has always been a significant factor in Christian theological reflection, but here it is not just a recalling of what God has done in history for salvation that is being encouraged but a linking of the readers' own history to those events. In this way the world of worship in Ephesians depends on its readers' experience of the transformation from then to now and of the grace of God which accomplished this change. Of course much has been written in recent years on the potential of story for theologizing.[5] Here all that needs to be underlined is that Ephesians suggests the fruitfulness of believers developing a story of their past, both as individuals and as a community, which relates it to the story of

[5] Cf. e.g. G. W. Stroup, *The Promise of Narrative Theology: Recovering the Gospel in the Church* (Atlanta, John Knox Press, 1981); D. Tracy, *The Analogical Imagination* (London, SCM, 1981), pp. 275–81, 296–8.

God's election of Israel and his actions in Christ. With its contrast schema it suggests too that that story will need to take account of discontinuity as well as continuity, doing justice to a negative past and the change which God's rescue act in Christ has effected.

In Ephesians the ethical exhortation builds on and arises out of the motivation provided by the sense of gratitude evoked through the language of worship and anamnesis. This provides a reminder that in Christian theologizing ethical deliberation, in the midst of its complexities, should never lose sight of the fact that ethics are first of all a thankful response to God's gracious initiative. They are a response which will always be more effective when inspired by celebration and affirmation of the realities and values, whose implications must now be lived out, in short, when they are the practice of praise.

## IDENTITY AND CALLING

When it comes to the content of Ephesians, contemporary Christians can immediately relate to its central concern of believers' distinctive identity. Indeed, so pervasive is the issue of identity in our culture that one might well suspect that our treatment has read it back into the letter. Our earlier discussion, particularly the rhetorical analysis of the letter, has claimed, however, that this is not the case, but rather that the discourse and its symbols indicate that the writer perceives the reinforcement of their identity to be his readers' main need.

Of the many analyses of the understanding of identity in our culture, one of the most perceptive is Charles Taylor's *Sources of the Self: the Making of the Modern Identity*,[6] in which he argues, in interaction with contrasting accounts where this is denied, that the sense of self is intimately related to a moral and spiritual vision of life, which needs to be articulated. Ephesians, as we have seen, articulates a Christian vision of existence in order to sustain and reinforce its readers' sense of identity. The

6 Cambridge University Press, 1989.

potential of such a reading of Ephesians for appropriation in the context of present-day discussions of identity can only be hinted at here through brief references to Taylor's work. As opposed to views of the self as disengaged, as neutral or as pure independent consciousness, he argues that 'in order to have a sense of who we are, we have to have a notion of how we have become, and of where we are going'.[7] These are, of course, the categories we found appropriate for our analysis of the thought of Ephesians in chapter 7. Both Ephesians 6 and Taylor find the image of standing within moral and spiritual conflict a telling one for identity. 'To know who I am is a species of knowing where I stand. My identity is defined by the commitments and identifications which provide the frame or horizon within which I can try to determine from case to case what is good, or valuable, or what ought to be done, or what I endorse or oppose. In other words, it is the horizon within which I am capable of taking a stand.'[8] Ephesians makes frequent use of the symbol of fullness for the goal of human existence. Taylor too sees the human aspiration for meaning as the search for fuller being and claims that 'this aspiration to fulness can be met ... by connecting one's life up with some greater reality or story'.[9] In Ephesians, what God has done in Christ provides this greater reality or story, and the Church, which is already the fullness of Christ and is to grow towards that fullness, is an essential frame of reference for believers' sense of identity, which is to be a communal one. Over against modern notions of highly independent individualism, Taylor asserts that 'the full definition of someone's identity ... involves not only his stand on moral and spiritual matters but also some reference to a defining community'.[10] In an interesting exploration Taylor also shows that central to modern notions of identity and crucial for any sense of the dignity of the self is the affirmation of ordinary life, the conviction that everyday living is not merely of infrastructural importance but can be 'the very centre of the

[7] *Sources of the Self*, p. 47.
[8] Ibid., p. 27.
[9] Ibid., p. 43.
[10] Ibid., p. 36.

good life'.[11] We have seen that Ephesians too affirms ordinary
life as the context for believers' distinctive sense of identity. In
its extended paraenesis and particularly its household code,
and in a way that distinguishes it from the historical Paul
(because of its longer term perspective on life in the world), it
anchors its cosmic vision firmly within everyday life so that, for
example, the relation between the cosmic Christ and the
Church underpins the importance of the marriage
relationship.

Unlike many contemporary discussions of self-identity, the
message of Ephesians for its readers is not narcissistic. Its
theological and Christological framework transforms issues of
the readers' identity into issues of their calling.[12] Their
identity is not autonomous or self-grounded but entirely
dependent on God's electing purpose actualized in his call.
Once identity is seen, as it is in Ephesians, in terms of calling
(cf. especially 1.18, 4.1, 4),[13] then the work of the develop-
mental theorist, James Fowler, also becomes fruitful for contemporary interpretation. His *Becoming Adult, Becoming Christian*[14] employs the concept of vocation or calling as an
overarching model for the development of an adult Christian
identity. In it he claims to be attempting to clarify not just the
idea of Christian vocation but the Christian understanding of
human vocation, which he defines not as a person's job, pro-
fession or career but as 'the response a person makes with his or
her total self to the address of God and to the calling to
partnership'.[15] It is extremely significant that in its perspective
on calling a major emphasis of Ephesians is on growth, maturing, progress toward a goal and that one of the designations of
that goal is 'the mature person' (4.13), with the stress on the

---

[11] Ibid., p. 13. For Taylor's tracing of the development of this conviction, see
pp. 211–302.
[12] Cf. also W. Brueggemann, 'Covenanting as Human Vocation', *Interpretation* 33
(1979), p. 125, who claims that a covenantal view of reality 'transposes all identity
questions into vocational questions'.
[13] See chapter 7, pp. 112–13 for the function of this notion as an overarching link
between the two halves of the letter.
[14] San Francisco, Harper & Row, 1984.
[15] Fowler, *Becoming Adult*, p. 95.

adulthood of this person in contrast to the instability of children (4.14).[16]

In Ephesians, as we have seen, the mature person is a corporate entity, the Church. Fowler too insists on 'the priority, in vocational existence, of community'[17] and asserts that 'there is no selfhood apart from community; no faith apart from community; no destiny and no vocation apart from community'.[18] For Fowler the goal of human development is God's universal commonwealth of love, this vocation is the secret entrusted to faith, and the Church is meant to proclaim and demonstrate this universal calling of humankind in anticipation.[19] Again, this is reminiscent of Ephesians with its message that the true human vocation is the calling to live as the community of the Church and thereby play a special role in God's purposes for the cosmos. These purposes are a mystery or secret disclosed to faith, involve the harmonious summing up of the cosmos in Christ and lead humanity to the experience of ultimate reality – the fullness of God – as all-embracing love (cf. 3.17–19). Unity and love in the Church is the pledge within history of the fulfilment of God's purposes. The bulk of Fowler's discussion tries to combine the best insights into the dynamics of personal adult development and an understanding of divine calling that is at the heart of Christian faith, and to show the liberating implications when such a view of vocation orchestrates a person's changing adult life structures.[20] It is a discussion which provides a suggestive context for a contemporary appropriation of the main thrust of Ephesians.

### GRACE AND POWER

As we have seen, Ephesians underlines heavily that its readers' identity and status are all of grace. Its talk of the gospel in terms

---

[16] For details, see Lincoln, *Ephesians*, pp. 256–8. The significance of Eph. 4.13 is recognized in passing by Fowler, *Becoming Adult*, p. 103.

[17] *Becoming Adult*, p. 112.

[18] Ibid., p. 113. Cf. also P. D. Hanson's major biblical theology of community developed under the rubric of calling, *The People Called: the Growth of Community in the Bible* (San Francisco, Harper & Row, 1986).

[19] *Becoming Adult*, p. 84.

[20] Cf. especially ibid., pp. 103–5, 137–8.

of the disclosure of the mystery is a clear reminder of the limitations of human knowledge and achievement. Experiential knowledge of God and therefore of one's self is shown to be ultimately dependent on the divine initiative in revelation. The writer could not be clearer that salvation has come freely, generously and undeservedly to a humanity bent on pursuing its own ends. That it is 'by grace' means that it has not originated from any human source but comes from God as a gift. That it is 'by faith' means that any human effort and, therefore, any pride or boasting are excluded (cf. 2.1–10). Essential to any appropriation of Ephesians is an experience of the grace of God in Christ whereby people know that their identity and sense of worth do not depend on any performance on their part but simply on having been accepted at the heart of reality as they are. It is on this basis that people receive God's call. The gospel of God's grace comes to them as a liberating word from outside their everyday experience, which they need to hear again and again, particularly in the face of experiences which seem to contradict it, and then dare to live their lives sustained by God's acceptance of them. The dynamic cycle of grace which moves through acceptance, sustenance and status to achievement is crucial to human well-being.[21]

Only from such a perspective can Ephesians' language of election be appropriated. Whatever the problems with the concept of election in the history of doctrine, whatever the fatalistic and deterministic distortions it has undergone, it expresses an essential part of Christian experience.[22] Talk of election occurs, significantly, in the context of thanksgiving (cf. 1.3–14) as part of an expression of gratitude for God's inexplicable grace, not as a logical deduction about the destiny of individuals based on the immutability of God's decrees. Those who know the grace of God in Christ feel compelled to say that the initiative in the matter of believing lies not with them but

[21] On this, see especially F. Lake, *Clinical Theology* (London, Darton, Longman and Todd, 1966), pp. 133–4.
[22] On the history of interpretation of election and predestination in Ephesians, see Schnackenburg, *Ephesians*, pp. 312–15.

with the one in whom they believe. They did not achieve faith by themselves and so they do not feel like congratulating themselves. Because the character of their experience is that of a gift, undeserved, the way they have to think of themselves is as those whom God has called or invited, in other words, elected.

The writer of Ephesians assumes that his readers have experienced not only the grace of God but also the power of God. Salvation is seen as an act of liberation, of transference with Christ from one sphere of power to another – from bondage to the sphere of the flesh, 'this world-age' and death to enjoyment of the new order of resurrection life and the heavenly realms (cf. 2.1–6), from enslavement to impurity, covetousness and idolatry to inheritance in the kingdom of Christ and God (cf. 5.3–5). Thinking in terms of opposing spheres of power can sometimes appear foreign to the contemporary interpreter. Yet a closer analysis reveals that all people, whether they are conscious of it or not, have a centring power in their lives that provides meaning and influences their attitudes, emotions and behaviour. Luke T. Johnson has a helpful discussion of Paul's notion of idolatry in terms of centres of power, making effective use of the phenomenon of addiction as the clearest example of enslavement to such a centre.[23] Whether the power at the centre of people's lives is another person, the state, the need for approval, their self-image, work or the pursuit of pleasure, if it is something other than the one ultimate Power, it becomes an idol that enslaves and produces compulsive behaviour. This is what Ephesians means by living 'according to this world-age ... in the passions of our flesh, carrying out the wishes of the flesh and thought'. Ephesians calls covetousness idolatry, because, refusing to acknowledge life and worth as a gift from God, lust makes some other desired object the centre of power.

But Ephesians also sees the resurrection and exaltation of Christ as the supreme demonstration of God's power, as inaugurating a new situation within history and its conflict of

[23] *Faith's Freedom* (Minneapolis, Fortress, 1990), pp. 61–7.

powers. Through their relationship to Christ believers are initiated into a new dominion, whose reality they are to appropriate. Again and again, whether it is expressed in terms of growth in unity, putting on the new person, living as children of light or taking up the whole armour of God, what believers are called on to do is to avail themselves of the resources that come from the new centre of power in their lives so that the distinctive pattern of behaviour that flows from this power can be produced. This is the force of the exhortation to be filled with the Spirit (5.18). The Spirit is the invisible go-between, who mediates the power of God and of Christ to believers. And they are exhorted to allow this centre of power to have the fullest control that they are conscious of in their lives, to open themselves up continually to the spiritual power who can enable them to live wisely and who can inspire their worship and thanksgiving. If idolatry and negative patterns of compulsive behaviour shape the identity of those under the old order, then it is thanksgiving that predominantly characterizes the identity of those who recognize the grace and power of the Creator at the centre of life (cf. 5.3, 4).

### THE CHURCH AND TRADITION

For Ephesians, identity is that of a person in community, and calling is to be part of a new humanity, the Church. The Church is the present focus of God's grace and power, the corporate context for thankfulness as a community of worship that recognizes that God is never the means to an end but that God is God. Obviously, the importance Ephesians attaches to the Church must be reckoned with in any contemporary appropriation, whatever the shortcomings of that Church in its manifestation in the various Christian bodies in our society and the attendant temptations to individualistic versions of Christianity.[24] What Ephesians primarily contributes to contemporary reflection on the Church through its various symbols and descriptions is a basis for theological self-understanding. Much

---

[24] On this, see D. E. Jenkins, 'The Impossibility and the Necessity of the Church', *Still Living with Questions* (London, SCM, 1990), pp. 145–51.

can be learned from sociological analysis of the Church as a social institution,[25] but, as Schnackenburg claims, 'A purely sociological view which only heeds the empirical shape of the Church (or churches) does not achieve the believing insight into the nature of "Church" without which it is impossible to understand the Church as a social entity.'[26] No viable ecclesiology can surrender the affirmation of the Apostles' Creed and the Nicene Creed about the one holy catholic and apostolic Church which this letter helped to shape.[27] At the same time, it would be a complete anomaly if belief in the one universal Church were ever to become an excuse for unwillingness on the part of Christians to commit themselves to one of its particular local manifestations.

In Ephesians the Church is not only a major part of the content of revelation (e.g. 3.6, 10; 5.32) but it is also the context of revelation (e.g. 1.9; 3.5, 21). The letter's Christological ecclesiology reflects a dialectic between Christ and the Church, which is equivalent to that between gospel and tradition, and is a reminder that it is in and through the Church that we possess the gospel about God's act of salvation in Christ. In particular, Ephesians sees it as the special task of ministers of the word to pass on the truth of the apostolic gospel in such a way as to edify the Church and lead it toward the unity of the faith. The importance of such teaching for the life of the Church must not be underestimated. The teaching office in the Catholic tradition has performed this function for its members and is one of its strengths, enabling it to speak authoritatively to its members in contrast to the fragmentation which often prevails within the Protestant tradition. At the same time, of course, the magisterium has frequently fallen into the trap of exaggerating its role and has exercised a repressive

---

[25] Cf. P. C. Hodgson, *Revisioning the Church* (Philadelphia, Fortress, 1988), pp. 64–8.

[26] *Ephesians*, p. 309.

[27] For excellent treatments of these marks of the Church, see H. Küng, *The Church* (London, Search Press, 1971), pp. 263–359; Hodgson, *Revisioning the Church*, pp. 37–44. R. E. Brown, *The Churches the Apostles Left Behind* (New York, Paulist, 1984), pp. 55–9, notes, however, two possible weaknesses which derive from Ephesians' stress on the holiness of the Church as the bride of Christ. It can lead to the tendency to cover up the Church's faults and makes it difficult to take seriously the possibility of reform.

and stultifying control which ignores the contribution of all believers.[28] The writer of Ephesians himself provides an excellent example of a teacher who both preserves and updates the apostolic gospel in the light of the ongoing experience of his readers. Through its own use of traditions, his letter demonstrates already within the canon the way in which tradition is a living and dynamic process through which the gospel of Christ is continually interpreted and actualized. What is needed in the contemporary Church is a similar teaching ministry which will nurture creative appropriations of Christian texts, provide theological articulation of what the Church is, foster ecumenical openness and raise consciousness about the Church's global role.[29]

### RECONCILIATION AND UNITY IN THE CHURCH

The vision of the Church in Ephesians is of a community of forgiving and accepting love based on its experience of God's forgiving and accepting love in Christ (cf. 4.32–5.2). The Church is a reconciled and reconciling community, the place in which both Jews and Gentiles and humanity and God have been reconciled to each other. It is the arena in which the results of Christ's peacemaking are to be seen in the one new person and the one body (cf. 2.14–16). The peace gained at the cost of Christ's death and realized in the Church is to be preserved and demonstrated (cf. 4.3) and proclaimed in the world (cf. 6.15).[30] What the writer believes has been achieved in the Church is the overcoming of the major division within humanity in the first century CE. That major division can be treated as a prototype of all divisions (cf. Gal. 3.28; Col. 3.11). If the Church in Ephesians stands for the overcoming of the division between Jews and Gentiles, it stands in the appropriation of contemporary readers for the overcoming of divi-

---

[28] For a good discussion of the strengths and weaknesses of the Catholic and Protestant traditions in this matter, see Schneiders, *The Revelatory Text*, pp. 81–6.
[29] Cf. Hodgson, *Revisioning the Church*, pp. 99–102.
[30] As E. Schillebeeckx, *Christ* (London, SCM, 1980), p. 217, puts it, 'the author of Ephesians dared to call the "community of God" the great *universal instrument of peace* in this world'.

sions caused by class, colour, wealth, gender, nationality or religious tradition. Anything less would be a denial of that nature of the Church which is axiomatic for Ephesians, yet even to make the assertion underlines how far the Church has to go to become what it is. Just how fundamental the unity of the Church is for this writer can be seen in 4.4–6 where monotheism is viewed as the source of that unity. The obvious corollary is that when the Church fails to maintain and express unity, it seriously undermines the credibility of its belief in the one God.

Ephesians' main symbol for the Church is the body with its unity but diversity of contributions from each member, including the special contributions of ministers of the word. In their interdependence the contributions of all are necessary for growth towards the unity the body already possesses. It is clear that this vision of the unity of the Church sees the body as one universal entity, but there is no way of knowing precisely how the writer would have related this vision to the concrete reality of the life of the churches in his own time. We should in all probability assume that he was well aware of the tensions, conflicts and divisions within early Christianity which we see reflected in the Pauline letters and that nevertheless he still held out as the ideal the unity of the whole Christian movement of his day. The tension between Ephesians' ideal for the Church and the fragmentary and ambiguous embodiment of this in actual churches has led theologians to make distinctions such as that between the invisible and the visible Church. Perhaps a better distinction is to talk of the essence of the Church, uniting the ideal and the real, and the historical expression of this essence which is always partial, incomplete and broken.[31]

This is certainly not the place for any extensive discussion of the present state of ecumenical endeavours. In the light of Ephesians one can only assert both the validity and necessity of such endeavours and claim that its message remains invaluable as a major energizing resource for them. Of the many treat-

---

[31] For an elaboration of this distinction, see the illuminating discussion of Hodgson, *Revisioning the Church*, pp. 52–63, 104–5.

ments of ecumenism that could be mentioned, Oscar Cullmann's is one that is suggestive because of its attempt to relate
a New Testament perspective on unity in charismatic diversity
to the ecumenical task. He recognizes that in the New Testament diversity is as fundamental to the Church as is unity, and
therefore argues that ecumenicity will not mean uniformity but
will allow for the distinctive gifts that have been given to each
of the Christian traditions. 'Each has been given grace' (Eph.
4.6) can be extended by analogy, so that the grace given to
each of the Christian traditions can be seen to be potentially
enriching for the unity of the whole. The converse of this is that
distortions of this grace will be potential hindrances to the
unity of the whole.[32] Cullmann, sensitive to the obstacles to
unity presented by official Roman Catholic claims that its
church alone possesses and guarantees the fullness of the gospel
and that the papacy is the divinely legitimated guarantee of
unity, wonders whether it is possible for the Roman Catholic
church to enter into a union of churches that was not simply a
merger into its own organization without giving up what it
views as a foundational element in its identity. He therefore
proposes that a non-utopian goal would be the formation of a
new general ecumenical council which would not involve a
merger into one structure but allow Eastern Orthodox, Roman
Catholic and Protestant churches to retain their own structures. This conciliar organization would enable co-operation
in areas which did not encroach on the authority of each
tradition. It would not itself be the Church as the body of
Christ but would express unity by bringing to awareness that
in the individual churches that participated in it the one
universal Church was present.[33]

Cullmann's proposal would certainly be a step forward, but
for him this federal arrangement is not an interim goal but the
'ultimate goal of all our strivings toward unity'.[34] Realism
rather than utopianism, is required, but whether such an

[32] Cf. O. Cullmann, *Unity through Diversity*, tr. M. E. Boring (Philadelphia, Fortress,
1988), pp. 16–22.
[33] Ibid., pp. 49–65.
[34] Ibid., p. 15.

arrangement does sufficient justice to the vision of Ephesians must be doubted. In the terms of Cullmann's own discussion, it appears to succumb too easily to the distortions of grace within the Roman Catholic tradition. Moving on from a federal council for separated churches to a single communion, in which radical diversity still flourishes, must be the long-term goal.[35] This will require all churches, but especially the Roman Catholic church, with its official view that it has been entrusted with the very fullness of grace and truth, to take seriously the 'not yet' in regard to the Church that is retained in Ephesians. It will require also the patient and persistent exercise of the qualities called for in the letter's own exhortation about unity – a loving tolerance of those with whom one differs (4.2, 3), which does not, however, become a sentimental relativism, because it endeavours to speak the truth in love (4.15).

## COSMIC AND UNIVERSAL PERSPECTIVE

Despite the focus on the Church in Ephesians, that Church is not allowed simply to be preoccupied with its own concerns.[36] It is called to a distinctive life of holiness in the midst of its surrounding culture, and, according to the writer, the values the Church lives by are as opposed to that culture's values as light is opposed to darkness. The determining of the boundaries between the Church and the world is a task that each generation of Christians has to perform for its own time and place, yet it is not one that should lead to any isolationism in relation to the world. Instead, in Ephesians it is suggested that as the Church in the midst of society is true to its identification with the light of the risen Christ, so that light is able to transform any surrounding darkness (cf. 5.11–14). This optimistic note is in line with the letter's universal vision. God is the cosmic father of all (cf. 3.15), and through the cosmic Christo-

---

[35] Cf. also Hodgson, *Revisioning the Church*, pp. 91–2.
[36] *Contra* Beker, *Heirs of Paul*, p. 111, Ephesians does not 'entail a concept of the church that celebrates its own salvation so much that it disregards the rest of the world'. For a good summary of the relationship between the Church and the world in Ephesians, see Schnackenburg, *Ephesians*, p. 308.

logy, which sees the Church's head as head over all and the one who fills the Church as filling all things (cf. 1.22, 23), a continuity between the realm of salvation and the realm of creation is established. As it is drawn into worship of the one Lord of all and the one God and Father of all (cf. 4.5, 6), the Church senses its solidarity with the whole human family which derives from the same Parent and is intended for the same destiny of universal harmony. The whole of created reality becomes the Church's legitimate concern, and the Church symbolizes the realization of the possibilities inherent in God's purposes for all creation, as it is called to be the paradigm of the cosmic unity which is their goal (cf. 1.10; 3.10). Here is a clear mandate for Christians to be 'world Christians', as they 'think globally and act locally' in demonstrating God's purposes for our one world, whether in the work of achieving a fair share of its resources between the nations of the North and those of the South or in the dialogue with other world religions or in the cause of healing for the environment. Global politics, inter-faith dialogue and ecology have everything to do with the cosmic harmony which is the vision of Ephesians for the future.[37]

### THE COSMIC POWERS

In its cosmic perspective Ephesians shares the world view of its day about the existence of evil spiritual powers in the heavenly realms. There has been a variety of recent attempts, of which the most extensive and impressive has been the work of Walter Wink,[38] to appropriate the treatment of the powers in the Pauline corpus for contemporary theology. But at this point it seems necessary to me to draw a clear line between exegesis and appropriation. The popular demythologizing of the powers whereby they represent the structures of human society may

---

[37] Schillebeeckx, *Christ*, p. 196, can go so far as to claim, 'If any book lays the foundation for a political theology in the New Testament, it is Ephesians, though the author himself does not see through its historical consequences or implications'.

[38] Cf. his *Naming the Powers* and *Unmasking the Powers* (Philadelphia, Fortress, 1986). A third volume, *Engaging the Powers*, is forthcoming.

well be a helpful reinterpretation, but it is precisely that, a reinterpretation. Despite Wink's argument that in the New Testament the powers do not have a separate spiritual existence but are the inner or spiritual essence of an institution or state,[39] there can be little doubt that in Ephesians they are seen as supernatural spiritual beings.[40] On the other hand, even if one might be prepared to see some personal centre of evil behind occult manifestations or to question whether the modern Western world view has said the last word about the nature of reality, this does not justify a straightforward appropriation of the cosmic demonology of Ephesians for contemporary theology.[41] Instead, Wink's misreading of Ephesians in its first century context may well turn out to be the most useful reading of it for our own context, enabling an analogy to be drawn between the cosmic principalities and powers and the systems, structures and institutions of our own day, which, within and beyond them, have a driving force for good or evil that is more than the sum of the effects of any individuals who may represent them or of any of their tangible manifestations. Such a view provides a perspective which recognizes that the struggle against unjust social structures is not against flesh and blood but involves a spiritual dimension for which spiritual resources are necessary.

### THE CHURCH AND ISRAEL

The need to distinguish between exegesis and appropriation applies equally to any appeal to Ephesians for support in the delicate task of Jewish–Christian dialogue. One example of such an appeal is the work of Markus Barth, who believes that there is one people of God, Israel, of which Gentile Christians have also become members, so that Jews and Christians are members of the same family. In his book *The People of God*, Barth claims that the perspective of Ephesians 2 is that 'the

[39] Cf. esp. *Naming the Powers*, pp. 104–5.
[40] Cf. Lincoln, *Ephesians*, pp. 63–5; C. Arnold, *Ephesians, Power and Magic* (Cambridge University Press, 1989), pp. 41–56 and *Powers of Darkness* (Leicester, Inter-Varsity Press, 1992), pp. 89–99, 198–201.
[41] *Pace* Arnold, *Powers of Darkness*, pp. 167–217.

church of Jews and Gentiles has no right to let herself be called "body of the Messiah (or, of Christ)", nor to call herself "people of God", unless she recognizes and acknowledges that she is participating in the history and community of the Jews'.[42] On the basis of the teaching of Ephesians he asserts that 'the church, the synagogue, and the State of Israel, as well as all secularized Jews, belong in this people and carry its name' and that the church will not witness to the Jews, but the Jews and the church will witness to the rest of the world.[43] However laudable any recognition that the relationship between the Church and the Jewish people should be part of the ecumenical task and however desirable any hope for rapprochement between Christianity and its parent religion, it seems undeniable to me that Barth's view represents a drastically mistaken interpretation of Ephesians 2.11–22 in its original context. The unity of which the passage speaks is not one between Christians and Jews, the Church and the synagogue, but one between Gentile Christians and Jewish Christians in the one body of the Church. The Gentile readers' previous disadvantages have been reversed not by their being incorporated into Israel, even into a remnant of Jewish Christians, but by their having become part of a new community which transcends the categories of Jew and Gentile, a new creation, not simply a merger of the former groupings. Granted that the writer still uses the language of an elect people in 2.19, this category has been transformed. Gentile Christians no longer lack a commonwealth, yet this is not because they are now part of the commonwealth of Israel, but because they are fellow-citizens with all the saints in the Church. The clear emphasis is on a decisive discontinuity between the old and the new peoples of God. The inescapable conclusion is that this passage depicts the Church in terms of a new third entity, a third race which transcends the old ethnic and religious identities of both Jew and Gentile.[44]

---

[42] Cf. *The People of God* (Sheffield, JSOT, 1983), p. 47.
[43] Ibid., pp. 71–2.
[44] For a fuller exegetical justification of this reading, see Lincoln, *Ephesians*, pp. 134–65.

It is, however, equally inescapable that the 'third race' notion reflected in Ephesians frequently led later to a deplorable denial of any continuing validity for Israel as a people.[45] It might, therefore, well be argued that the perspective of Ephesians is no longer of any help for a sensitive post-holocaust Christian theology. On the other hand, it might be that, as one of the variety of emphases within the tension between continuity and discontinuity which characterizes the relation of the Church to Israel in the New Testament, the stance of Ephesians still has a contribution to make. Any worthwhile dialogue between Christianity and Judaism will not be one in which Christians abandon the conviction of Ephesians that in Christ God has done something decisively new for human salvation and has made possible a human community that transcends ethnic boundaries. And although the hopes of the Paul of Romans, still in anguished interaction with Judaism, may be more congenial to Christians engaged in rapprochement between the Church and the Jewish people, Ephesians reflects a later stage when events appear to have passed his hopes by, and when the Christian movement has become an independent and predominantly Gentile phenomenon. It may therefore provide a check on any present day utopian hopes about the outcome of Jewish–Christian dialogue or about the possibility of retrieving a situation where Christianity could be seen as a renewal movement within Judaism.[46] The contribution of Ephesians is not, however, entirely negative. The hope implicit in its view that the grace of God in Christ and the reconciling work of Christ have overcome Gentile Christians' former unbelief and alienation is that they can and will overcome the unbelief and alienation of others. After all, Ephesians sees the unity of Jewish Christians and Gentile Christians within the Church as but the first step toward the bringing of

---

[45] Cf. W. Rader, *The Church and Racial Hostility* (Tübingen, Mohr, 1978), pp. 156, 171–3, 228–34. Cf. also Schnackenburg, *Ephesians*, pp. 321–5 on the history of interpretation of the Church's relation to Israel in Ephesians.

[46] From the Jewish side, J. Neusner, *Jews and Christians* (London, SCM, 1991), insists that, if genuine dialogue is to occur, it must be recognized first of all that Judaism and Christianity are two different religions and not simply two versions of one religion.

the whole cosmos into harmony in Christ. The Church points beyond itself to a more complete future salvation. On this side of the eschaton, however, an appropriation of Ephesians may suggest that there is room in the conversation with Judaism for Christians to witness to their experience of the grace of God in Christ and its universal scope, though any such witness will need to be in a spirit of repentance and love that speaks louder than words.[47]

MARRIAGE

A more complete appropriation of Ephesians would need to deal both positively with its view of the Church as the context for ethical discernment and character formation and critically with a number of the specific ethical stances taken by its writer, including his prohibition of anger and of all talk about sexual vices and his acceptance of slavery. There is only space, however, to make some brief comments about his extensive treatment of marriage. Some writers are convinced that Eph. 5.21–33 provides the model for all Christian marriage,[48] while others are clearer about its shortcomings in the light of a feminist reading.[49] As we have seen, the writer's call to mutual submission and his depiction of the husband's exercise of headship in terms of loving sacrifice gave the traditional roles in the patriarchal household a different dynamic. But the analogy with Christ and the Church should not lure interpreters into seeing his paraenesis as a universal prescription for marriage through the ages. The situation cannot be improved by a revisionist exegesis which attempts to conform the passage to modern sensitivities and to make the writer an egalitarian before his time, either by treating the injunction to mutual submission as a radical critique of all that follows or by redefining subordination or by emptying the concept of headship of

---

[47] For a fuller statement of this proposal, see Lincoln, 'The Church and Israel in Ephesians 2', *CBQ* 49 (1987), pp. 621–4.

[48] Cf. e.g. Barth, *Ephesians*, esp. pp. 715, 753.

[49] Cf. e.g. E. Schüssler Fiorenza, *In Memory of Her* (New York, Crossroad, 1983), pp. 266–70.

all suggestions of authority. The writer's use of the analogy of Christ and the Church reveals that his point of view is pervasively androcentric. It is assumed, for instance, that the model of Christ is for the husband and the model of the Church for the wife and, in line with this, that love is to be expected of the husband and the wife can be likened to her husband's body, but not vice-versa.

Ephesians 5.21–33 is best appropriated by attempting to do what its writer has done, that is, to bring to bear on the marriage conventions of the day what is held to be the heart of the Christian message. This is not so easy where family structures in society are themselves in flux, but those who regard love and justice as at the heart of Christian ethics will want to work out a view of marriage where both partners are held in equal regard, where justice will require that traditional male dominance cannot be tolerated, and where love ensures that the relationship does not degenerate into a sterile competition for control. Instead of assigning love to the husband and submission to the wife, a contemporary appropriation may well build on the opening exhortation of the paraenesis in 5.21 by emphasizing a mutuality of loving submission. Submission and love can in this way be seen as two sides of the same coin – unselfish service of one's partner, challenging the view of relationships as purely romantic or sexual or simply contracts of convenience. Although the hierarchical elements in the paraenesis may be rejected in the light of the full implications of the gospel, the notion of the permanent 'one flesh' union of Gen. 2.24, which underlies the writer's exhortation to husbands as well as serving as the vehicle for his distinctive interpretation of the relation between Christ and the Church, is likely to remain the Christian ideal for marriage, providing the secure context for commitment, trust and growth. Such an ideal can still be seen to have a 'sacramental' dimension, as marital union reflects in its own way the unity that is God's purpose for all humanity and the cosmos and that is at present realized in the relationship between Christ and the Church.

## SIGNIFICANT OMISSIONS

Given the particular purposes of all the New Testament documents, it would be unrealistic to expect any one of them to
contain all the emphases that one might wish to find. Ephesians
mentions only in passing the matter of care for the poor and
needy (cf. 4.28), and somewhat surprisingly does not mention
at all the Lord's Supper among the aspects of the Church's
unity. More significant, especially in comparison with Paul, is
the lack of a profound theology of the cross that sees in Christ's
death God's identification with human weakness and suffering.
Instead the stress is on the power of God at work in Christ's
resurrection and exaltation. Correspondingly, union with
Christ in his resurrection and exaltation rather than suffering
or dying with Christ dominates the letter's perspective on
Christian existence. The one mention of suffering is as part of
the image of the imprisoned apostle Paul. Suffering is not
mentioned as part of the readers' experience; instead, Paul's
suffering is said to result in their glory (3.13). One cannot
therefore turn to Ephesians for a compelling treatment of the
weakness, ambiguities and anguish that are an inherent part of
the tension between the 'already' and the 'not yet' of Christian
existence.

When one sets this lack alongside the letter's stress on the
exalted status of believers and the exalted role of the Church,
potential dangers for the appropriation of Ephesians, which
have not always been avoided in the history of interpretation,
can readily be seen. There is the danger that a vision of the
special place of the Church in God's purposes and of the
enabling power and victory of Christ will become triumphalis-
tic if it loses touch with human weakness and identification
with the death of Christ. There is also the danger that its
accompanying doxology will become complacent if it loses
touch with pain and suffering. It must be said, however, that
these charges cannot be fairly levelled against Ephesians in its
original context. Its message was meant to boost the confidence
of readers who had an insufficient sense of their identity and
was intended to produce not self-congratulation or arrogance

but a recognition of and humble gratitude for the magnificent achievement of God's grace on their behalf. Its doxology was to issue from those who were still profoundly conscious of a past in which they had been in bondage and deserving of God's judgement and of the transformation that God's grace and power had effected. Modern readers need to remain alert to the consequences and temptations that can result once Ephesians is loosed from such a context.

## HOPE

Despite its openness to abuse, this letter's dominant doxological vision of Christian existence and of the Church and its unity in a cosmic setting remains both necessary and persuasive, particularly when contemporary Christians become discouraged, are tempted to succumb to an individualistic piety, feel insignificant or lose their sense of identity and purpose. Indeed, it could well be argued that those who are not tempted to feel discouraged or insignificant have not yet sensed the scope of the calling and hope to which Ephesians invites its readers. The prayer of 1.17, 18 is that believers' eyes might be opened so that they know what is the hope of God's calling. The one hope that belongs to their calling (4.4) is not an individual and private one but the hope of a transformed cosmos, of a world that is unified and reconciled, where hostile powers out to fragment, disintegrate and produce alienation have been pacified and where all are brought together in harmony through what God has done in Christ (1.10). In the vision of Ephesians the existence of the Church, in which Jews and Gentiles have become one, is the tangible reminder to the alienating forces at work in the world that God is going to make good on his purposes for cosmic unity (cf. 3.5, 6, 10). The Church and its unity is the evidence for this assured hope.

The most likely and reasonable reaction to this central assertion of the letter is disbelief and derision. Yet any response of Christian faith needs to be one not of cynicism but of realism. People need hope to brace them and to give their lives coherence, and the ultimate hope of Ephesians remains compelling.

Reflection on the place of the Church in such a hope may be helped if we allow the letter's vision of the Church's unity to stand alongside not only the reality of fragmentation and division in and among the churches of today but also the similar reality in the earliest stages of the Church's life. As we have claimed, the writer was presumably not completely unaware of the tensions, conflicts and divisions that had plagued Paul's mission. Nevertheless, he perceived that in and through these less than perfect developments something substantial had taken place, and on this he builds his vision of the one Church, which at the same time functions as a call for it to become what it is. Putting Ephesians in context can serve as a reminder to contemporary readers that God can achieve his purposes through failure and broken dreams, but sharing the vision will keep them dissatisfied with anything short of its fulfilment.

In a poem reflecting on the place of the Church in society and beginning with words from Ephesians 2, T. S. Eliot went on to write,

> What life have you if you have not life together?
> There is no life that is not in community,
> And no community not lived in praise of GOD.[50]

Ephesians indeed issues an invitation for people to realize their true identity in a life in the community of praise that is the Church. Its idealized visionary depiction is meant to help its readers see their identity and calling in a new light, to open up new possibilities and to beckon them closer to achieving these. Sharing its vision of the Church's calling with its one hope for a world in harmony will mean living out the consequences of such a calling (4.1). The writer is clear that this will mean, above all, sparing no effort to maintain the unity of the Spirit (4.3) and that the essential quality needed is accepting love (4.2). The vision of Ephesians can function as a powerful incentive for hope rather than despair, because the magnitude of the calling it describes and of the commitment it requires is

---

[50] 'Choruses from "The Rock" 1934' in *The Complete Poems and Plays* (London, Faber & Faber, 1969), p. 152.

matched by the magnitude of the God with whom Christians co-operate in their calling. The God whose resources exceed anything humans can ask for or even imagine (3.20) is therefore well able to take up the Church's very imperfect and fragmented responses to his calling in achieving his purposes of unity and love for all.

# Guide to further reading – Colossians

## COMMENTARIES

The most useful, fuller commentaries for the student wishing commentaries in English include:

Bruce, F. F., *The Epistles to the Colossians, to Philemon, and to the Ephesians*, NICNT, Grand Rapids, Eerdmans, 1984; cf. also Bruce, F. F. and Simpson, E. K., *Commentary on the Epistles to the Ephesians and the Colossians*, NICNT, Grand Rapids, Eerdmans, 1957.

Lohse, E., *Colossians and Philemon*, Hermeneia, Philadelphia, Fortress, 1971; ET of MeyerK 9/2, Göttingen, Vandenhoeck & Ruprecht, 1968[14].

Martin, R. P., *Colossians: the Church's Lord and the Christian's Liberty*, Exeter, Paternoster, 1972.

*Colossians and Philemon*, NCB, London, Oliphants, 1974).

Moule, C. F. D., *The Epistles to the Colossians and to Philemon*, CGTC, Cambridge University Press, 1958.

O'Brien, P. T., *Colossians, Philemon*, WBC 44, Waco, Word, 1982.

Pokorný, P., *Colossians: a Commentary*, Peabody MA, Hendrickson, 1991; ET of THKNT 10/1, Berlin, Evangelische Verlagsanstalt, 1987.

Schweizer, E., *The Letter to the Colossians: a Commentary*, London, SPCK, 1982; ET of EKKNT, Zürich, etc., Benziger/Neukirchen, Neukirchener, 1976.

Among older commentaries in English that are still worth consulting the following may be mentioned:

Abbott, T. K., *Ephesians and Colossians*, ICC, Edinburgh, Clark, 1897.

Lightfoot, J. B., *Saint Paul's Epistles to the Colossians and to Philemon*, London, Macmillan, 1884[7].

Among briefer recent commentaries in English are:
Caird, G. B., *Paul's Letters from Prison*, New Clarendon Bible, London, Oxford University Press, 1976.
Houlden, J. L., *Paul's Letters from Prison (Philippians, Colossians, Philemon and Ephesians)*, Pelican NT Comms, Harmondsworth, Penguin, 1970.
Wright, N. T., *Colossians and Philemon*, Tyndale NT Comms, London, Inter-Varsity, 1987.

Particularly important recent commentaries available only in languages other than English include
Gnilka, J., *Der Kolosserbrief*, HTKNT 10/1, Freiburg, etc., Herder, 1980.

## OTHER WORKS

### BIBLIOGRAPHICAL

Further bibliographies may be found in most commentaries and in:
Ernst, J., 'Kolosserbrief', in *TRE*, vol. 19, Berlin, de Gruyter, 1989, pp. 370–6.
Schenk, W., 'Der Kolosserbrief in der neueren Forschung (1945–1985)', in *ANRW*, 2, 25.4, Berlin/New York, de Gruyter, 1987, pp. 3327–64.
Schweizer, E., 'Zur neueren Forschung am Kolosserbrief (seit 1970)', in *Theologische Berichte*, 5 (1976), pp. 163–91, repr. in Schweizer, *Neues Testament und Christologie im Werden: Aufsätze*, Göttingen, Vandenhoeck & Ruprecht, 1982, pp. 122–49.

The wealth of literature on the Christological hymn (Col 1.15–20) is almost infinite – see the bibliographies in J.-N. Aletti, *Colossiens 1,15–20: genre et exégèse du texte; fonction de la thématique sapientielle*, AnBib 91, Rome, Biblical Inst., 1981; P. Benoit, 'L'hymne christologique de Col 1,15–20: jugement critique sur l'état de recherches', in *Christianity, Judaism and Other Greco-Roman Cults: Studies for Morton Smith at Sixty*, SJLA 12, ed. J. Neusner, Leiden, Brill, 1975, vol. 1, pp. 226–63; C. Burger, *Schöpfung und Versöhnung: Studien zum liturgischen Gut im Kolosser- und Epheserbrief*, WMANT 46, Neukirchen-Vluyn, Neukirchener, 1975; H. J. Gabathuler, *Jesus Christus, Haupt der Kirche – Haupt der Welt: der Christushymnus Colosser 1,15–20 in der theologischen Forschung der letzten 130 Jahre*, ATANT 45, Zürich/Stuttgart, Zwingli, 1965.

The following works devoted to various other aspects of Colossians may also be singled out as particularly useful:

Crouch, J. E., *The Origin and Intention of the Colossian Haustafel*, Göttingen, Vandenhoeck & Ruprecht, 1972.
Francis, F. O. and Meeks, W. A. (eds.), *Conflict at Colossae*, SBLSBS 4, Cambridge MA, Scholars, 1975 – a collection of essays by a number of scholars (G. Bornkamm, Dibelius, Francis, Lightfoot, S. Lyonnet).
Kiley, M., *Colossians as Pseudepigraphy*, Sheffield, JSOT, 1986.

# Guide to further reading – Ephesians

## COMMENTARIES

The two most recent detailed commentaries in English are:
Lincoln, A. T., *Ephesians*, WBC 42, Dallas, Word, 1990.
Schnackenburg, R., *The Epistle to the Ephesians*, Edinburgh, Clark, 1991. ET of *Der Brief an die Epheser*, EKK 10, Zürich, Benzinger, 1982.
The former has a more extensive discussion of introductory issues and more thorough exegesis and interaction with recent scholarship. The latter contains valuable sketches of the history of interpretation of key themes.

Other commentaries in English that are worth consulting include:
Barth, M., *Ephesians*, AB 34 – 2 vols., New York, Doubleday, 1974.
Bruce, F. F., *The Epistles to the Colossians, to Philemon, and to the Ephesians*, NICNT, Grand Rapids, Eerdmans, 1984.
Foulkes, F., *The Epistle of Paul to the Ephesians*, TNTC, Leicester, IVP, 1989.
Martin, R. P., *Ephesians, Colossians, Philemon*, Interpretation, Atlanta, John Knox, 1991.
Mitton, C. L., *Ephesians*, NCB, London, Oliphants, 1976.

Among older commentaries in English that are still worth consulting are:
Abbott, T. K., *A Critical and Exegetical Commentary on the Epistles to the Ephesians and to the Colossians*, ICC, Edinburgh, Clark, 1897.
Eadie, J. A., *A Commentary on the Greek Text of the Epistle of Paul to the Ephesians*, Edinburgh, Clark, 1883³.
Meyer, H. A. W., *Critical and Exegetical Handbook to the Epistle to the Ephesians and the Epistle to Philemon*, tr. W. P. Dickson, Edinburgh, Clark, 1880.

Robinson, J. A., *St Paul's Epistle to the Ephesians*, London, Macmillan, 1904[4].
Scott, E. F., *The Epistles to the Colossians, to Philemon, and to the Ephesians*, MNTC, London, Hodder and Stoughton, 1930.
Westcott, B. F., *St Paul's Epistle to the Ephesians*, London, Macmillan, 1906.

Important recent commentaries in languages other than English include:
Gnilka, J., *Der Epheserbrief*, HTKNT, Freiburg, Herder, 1971.
Bouttier, M., *L'Épître de saint Paul aux Éphésiens*, CNT, Geneva, Labor et Fides, 1991.

## OTHER WORKS

### BIBLIOGRAPHICAL

Further bibliographies may be found in the recent commentaries and in:
Merkel, H., 'Der Epheserbrief in der neueren exegetischen Diskussion', *ANRW* 2.25.4, Berlin/New York, de Gruyter, 1987, pp. 3156–246.

### AUTHORSHIP AND SETTING

Arnold, C. E., *Ephesians: Power and Magic*, Cambridge University Press, 1989.
Best, E., 'Recipients and Title of the Letter to the Ephesians: Why and When the Designation "Ephesians"?' *ANRW* 25.2.4, Berlin/New York, de Gruyter, 1987, pp. 3247–79.
Fischer, K. M., *Tendenz und Absicht des Epheserbriefes*, Göttingen, Vandenhoeck & Ruprecht, 1973.
MacDonald, M. Y., *The Pauline Churches*, Cambridge University Press, 1988.
Meade, D. G., *Pseudonymity and Canon*, Tübingen, Mohr, 1986.
Mitton, C. L., *The Epistle to the Ephesians*, Oxford, Clarendon Press, 1951.
Roon, A. van, *The Authenticity of Ephesians*, Leiden, Brill, 1974.

### ASPECTS OF THEOLOGY

Much of the extended discussion of theological issues in Ephesians is in German and so some of these important works are listed below.

Students should also consult the brief treatments in Lincoln, *Ephesians*, pp. lxxxvii–xcvii on 'The Thought of Ephesians', and in Schnackenburg, *Ephesians*, pp. 293–310 on 'The Church in the Epistle to the Ephesians'.

Adai, J., *Der Heilige Geist als Gegenwart Gottes in den einzelnen Christen, in der Kirche und in der Welt*, Frankfurt, Peter Lang, 1985.

Arnold, C. E., *Ephesians: Power and Magic*, Cambridge University Press, 1989, pp. 123–66.

Brown, R. E., *The Churches the Apostles Left Behind*, New York, Paulist Press, 1984, pp. 47–60.

Corley, B., 'The Theology of Ephesians', SWJT 22 (1979), pp. 24–38.

Dahl, N. A., 'Interpreting Ephesians: Then and Now', *CurTM* 5 (1978), pp. 133–43.

Halter, H., *Taufe und Ethos: Paulinische Kriterien für das Proprium christlicher Moral*, Freiburg, Herder, 1977.

Lindemann, A., *Die Aufhebung der Zeit: Geschichtsverständnis und Eschatologie im Epheserbrief*, Gütersloh, Gerd Mohn, 1975.

Lona, H. E., *Die Eschatologie im Kolosser- und Epheserbrief*, Würzburg, Echter Verlag, 1984.

MacDonald, M. Y., *The Pauline Churches*, Cambridge University Press, 1988, pp. 85–158.

Martin, R. P., *Reconciliation: a Study of Paul's Theology*, London, Marshall, 1981, pp. 157–98.

Meeks, W. A., 'In One Body: the Unity of Humankind in Colossians and Ephesians', in *God's Christ and His People*, ed. J. Jervell and W. A. Meeks, Oslo, Universitets Vorlaget, 1977, pp. 209–21.

Merklein, H., *Das kirchliche Amt nach dem Epheserbrief*, Munich, Kösel, 1973.
    'Paulinische Theologie in der Rezeption des Kolosser- und Epheserbriefes', in *Paulus in den neutestamentlichen Spätschriften*, ed. K. Kertelge, Freiburg, Herder, 1981, pp. 25–69.

Steinmetz, F.-J., *Protologische Heilszuversicht: die Strukturen des soteriologischen und christologischen Denkens in Kolosser- und Epheserbrief*, Frankfurt, Josef Knecht, 1969.

Usami, K., *Somatic Comprehension of Unity: the Church in Ephesus*, Rome, Biblical Institute Press, 1983.

Wild, R. A., '"Be Imitators of God": Discipleship in the Letter to the Ephesians', in *Discipleship in the New Testament*, ed. F. Segovia, Philadelphia, Fortress, 1985, pp. 127–43.

# Index – Colossains

## References

EARLY CHRISTIAN WRITERS

OTHER GRAECO-ROMAN
WRITERS

## Subjects

## Authors

# Index – Ephesians

## References

## Subjects

## Authors